# "Lemme Tell You a Story"

# "Lemme Tell You a *Story*"

## Memoirs of Rev. Msgr. Allen J. Roy

by
Fr. Allen J. Roy

authorHOUSE®

AuthorHouse™
1663 Liberty Drive
Bloomington, IN 47403
www.authorhouse.com
Phone: 1-800-839-8640

© 2012 by Fr. Allen J. Roy. All rights reserved.

No part of this book may be reproduced, stored in a retrieval system, or transmitted by any means without the written permission of the author.

Published by AuthorHouse   10/30/2012

ISBN: 978-1-4772-5391-5 (sc)
ISBN: 978-1-4772-6472-0 (hc)
ISBN: 978-1-4772-6473-7 (e)

Library of Congress Control Number: 2012915967

Any people depicted in stock imagery provided by Thinkstock are models, and such images are being used for illustrative purposes only.
Certain stock imagery © Thinkstock.

This book is printed on acid-free paper.

Because of the dynamic nature of the Internet, any web addresses or links contained in this book may have changed since publication and may no longer be valid. The views expressed in this work are solely those of the author and do not necessarily reflect the views of the publisher, and the publisher hereby disclaims any responsibility for them.

# FOREWORD

The background to these stories and their telling comes out of a consideration of my early life spent with my family and many memorable experiences of my priesthood.

When I was born in Hamburg, Louisiana, in August of 1929, we belonged to the Diocese of Alexandria. My father and mother moved from Hamburg, after a few years, to Mansura, also in Avoyelles Parish. In 1932 came my brother Gerard (Jerry), and a few years later my brother Kearn (born in New Roads), with my youngest brother Pat coming later, in 1945.

I was ordained a priest for the Archdiocese of New Orleans on June 5th, 1954, at St. Louis Cathedral by Bishop Abel Caillouet with the Marian Year Class. The Plauche family (Mom was Lucy Plauche) is pleased to have many priests and nuns in our family.

The Plauches are known as "raconteurs" or "story-tellers." And I have had a rich life with many friends who themselves bring along many interesting stories, providing colorful material of interest for classes, conversations, and homilies. These stories, both in French and English, have been so interesting that kinsfolk, friends, and parishioners have asked for them. This is the background out of which they come.

In 2003, we, at Holy Spirit parish in Algiers, arranged for the People Program, a part of the mission of the Sisters of St. Joseph, to use our campus as a satellite for the West

Bank of New Orleans. This began a great chapter in my life (and the lives of quite a few friends). It continues today, touching the lives of so many 50+ year old friends who attend the classes. Barbara Donlon, who led the "Story-Telling" class, encouraged me to tell the stories and then to write them. And it continues today.

As is usual in many stories, the further one goes into a narration, the more material surfaces, and soon, once I began writing, I had quite a number of stories written about my life as a Cajun and as a priest with years of ministry in the Church. Getting them into book form, without any particular order or connection between them, has been an enjoyment.

There are many friends in my past to whom I have much gratitude for their help, witting and unwitting, to me. In this endeavor and this book and our stories, I would first of all give thanks to Barbara Donlon and to Phyllis Robert who not only did the editing with her English expertise but who kept me encouraged and headed in the right direction. Finally, I am indebted to all those teachers who have gifted me with the love of words, of Scripture, and of priestly ministry. I am deeply grateful.

The next step will involve the assembly of a booklet and the publishing of these stories, to be given to family members and to the many friends who have asked for copies. The "polish" which real writers possess will not be the point of the stories, but we seek to provide material for thought and life, as we run into the ideas, feelings, beliefs, and reactions of the people I've met and journeyed with in our lives of faith together.

Allen Roy<br>
June 2012

# TABLE OF CONTENTS

Foreword .................................................................................... v

An Introduction—Why These Stories? ................................... 1
Story 1:    Turned Upside Down ............................................ 3
Story 2:    Mom And Her Car ................................................. 4
Story 3:    My Dad: A Surprising Encounter ......................... 7
Story 4:    Jimmy Navis—Guilt Without Fault ...................... 8
Story 5:    Vestiges Of The Past—My Cassock ................... 10
Story 6:    Different Intro To Violet ..................................... 12
Story 7:    A Joyful Day At Ordination ............................... 15
Story 8:    Storms A-Plenty .................................................. 17
Story 9:    Our "New Hard Times" ...................................... 19
Story 10:  Mom's Revenge ................................................... 22
Story 11:  A Boy And His Dog ............................................. 24
Story 12:  What Goes Around Comes Around .................. 26
Story 13:  Jerry And His '32 Chevy ..................................... 28
Story 14:  Pat—Smell Like Chanel No. 5 ........................... 30
Story 15:  Kearn, A Straight Arrow .................................... 32
Story 16:  Hurricane Betsy Stuff .......................................... 35
Story 17:  Generous Fun-Filled Souls: Richard/Marceline ... 38
Story 18:  Let's Go, The Fish Are Biting ............................. 40
Story 19:  50 Years—Ain't Gawd Good? ............................ 43
Story 20:  Special People—Sr. Paula Richard ................... 45
Story 21:  Holy Spirit Beginning ......................................... 48
Story 22:  Moving From The Mary Joseph Residence ..... 51
Story 23:  How Not To Make Up To Someone .................. 53
Story 24:  Meg And The Bogue ........................................... 55
Story 25:  Part A—Special People—Adley Alleman Roy ... 58
Story 25:  Part B—Special People—Jeanie Ortego Roy .... 60
Story 26:  A Gift ..................................................................... 63

| | | |
|---|---|---|
| Story 27: | Mom's Friend, Mrs. Bizette | 64 |
| Story 28: | Looking Toward The Seminary: Fr. Janssens | 66 |
| Story 29: | Grandpa And Grandma—The Praying Rabbit | 68 |
| Story 30: | This Old (Warm) House: | 69 |
| Story 31: | Dual Cross-Country Flying: | 72 |
| Story 32: | Young Priest Experiences Death | 74 |
| Story 33: | A Super-Nurse—Sr. Janie Quatman, Emd | 76 |
| Story 34: | Willy Meridier: From Soldier To Priest | 78 |
| Story 35: | Stories Priests Used To Tell | 79 |
| Story 36: | Chauvin Friends | 81 |
| Story 37: | Violet Friends: Mrs. Perez And Ruth Maloof | 84 |
| Story 38: | A Strange Irony | 86 |
| Story 39: | A Baffling Encounter: "Out Of The Blue" | 89 |
| Story 40: | The Strength Of Music For Me | 91 |
| Story 41: | "Bean," The Skunk | 94 |
| Story 42: | The Sweetest Words In The English Language | 97 |
| Story 43: | What Was He Thinking? | 99 |
| Story 44: | You Mix The Army, Homesickness, Uncertainty, Mardi Gras, And What Do You Get? | 100 |
| Story 45: | A Puzzlement: What To Do? | 103 |
| Story 46: | Strange And Different | 105 |
| Story 47: | "Ask And You Shall Receive . . ." (Luke's Gospel, 11:9) | 107 |
| Story 48: | "One Never Knows What He Will Find . . ." | 108 |
| Story 49: | Grandpa's Heritage | 109 |
| Story 50: | World War II—A High School Story | 111 |
| Story 51: | "The Difficult" | 113 |
| Story 52: | Listening And What It Takes | 114 |
| Story 53: | "I Wish I Had Listened . . ." | 116 |
| Story 54: | Scared | 118 |
| Story 55: | "Un Coeur Casse'?" | 119 |
| Story 56: | Something Lost | 121 |
| Story 57: | "The Fragrance Of Wooden Matches And Coal Smoke" | 123 |
| Story 58: | A Different Mother's Day | 125 |
| Story 59: | "A Home-Made Surprise Attack" | 127 |

| | | |
|---|---|---|
| Story 60: | A Treasure For Me And For Many: | 129 |
| Story 61: | What It Was Like To Enter The Seminary | 132 |
| Story 62: | Jesus, Born A Girl? | 135 |
| Story 63: | Having Your Ideas Trampled On | 136 |
| Story 64: | "A Wise Person—Seven Years Detached—Why Wise?" | 139 |
| Story 65: | Words, La Parole: How We Take Some Of God's Gifts So Much For Granted! | 141 |
| Story 66: | "A Great And Needed Kindness" | 142 |
| Story 67: | Thoughts On A Theme By John Donne: "No Man Is An Island": (1572-1631). | 145 |
| Story 68: | A Sibling, Me And Jerry: | 147 |
| Story 69: | "A Gift Lost Before I Really Received It" | 148 |
| Story 70: | A Day Never To Be Forgotten | 150 |
| Story 71: | ". . . what Was I Thinking . . . !?" | 152 |
| Story 72: | Life After Birth | 153 |
| Story 73: | A Total Surprise | 155 |
| Story 74: | An Event Or Book Which Changed My Life And Outlook | 157 |
| Story 75: | Best Friend, Growing Up: Still In Contact? | 159 |
| Story 76: | "Me And The 'Il Faut' Concept" | 161 |
| Story 77: | "You Knew You Were In Trouble When . . . ." | 163 |
| Story 78: | Another Threshold | 164 |
| Story 79: | A Great Sign Of Faith And Discipline | 166 |
| Story 80: | An Unusual Stance | 167 |
| Story 81: | "Ye Olde Hoof In Mouth" | 168 |
| Story 82: | "The 2011 Mississippi River Flood" | 170 |
| Story 83: | "Renovabis Faciem Terrae"? | 172 |

# AN INTRODUCTION—
# WHY THESE STORIES?

For several months, I was asked to write or make available stories of some of my experiences as a priest and pastor. At first, I really didn't want to do this—it sounded like braggadocio or bull-shooting, but I needed to become a "raconteur," as Cajuns say.

In 1978, with my Mom, I visited with my 93-year-old grandfather, George Roy, in a rest home in Mansura, and, all in French, Mom and I asked him some questions about his life and brought along a good tape recorder to get some answers to our questions. (I really knew very little about that period of his life). That was okay. Then, 2 years later, I did the same with Mom in her kitchen. These recordings sat in tape cassettes for 20 years, until Kenny Lannes, a Holy Spirit parishioner, told me that he could put this information on CD. When he did it, it was so interesting that it caused the family to want a copy to listen to and learn.

Then, people began to ask about stories that I used in homilies and wanted me to put them in some sort of order that they might enjoy hearing. Can you imagine? They wanted me to get some of those stolen stories that I had and used. Could I copy them and make them available for them to read? Oh, well, I let that idea sit until I tried to record them on a digital audio recorder.

In the People Program here at Holy Spirit, we have had a class called "Story-Telling" led by Barbara Donlon, a wonderful story-teller. She told me to try it. When I did, it went nowhere—"sterile" she called it, as it really was. I needed another way to do this—I wanted to have something to leave for the younger folks in my family. But it was a chore. Then, a Lifeline Screening test found that I had an aneurysm in the abdomen and needed surgery. So, I looked at that time of recuperation to try it. Also, the Story-telling class had begun to blossom. Why not take my life-experiences and tell the stories about individual people and my impressions of things which have happened in my life and ministry? And so it is.

Once I began these stories, it became easier and easier to write. Memories flowed, even if there were times in my life when, not only had I experienced pain, but also I didn't want to bruise anyone later on with recounting my feelings and thoughts. I had to be careful: after all, some things which fly out of Pandora's box should be for only some eyes to see (or read or hear)! My decisions. I do have great editors who will help me to discern the recounting and what possible stories to include.

I have no idea how all this will fly and where it's going. I feel that some of it was interesting at the time, but now, later, it may be only the musings of un vieu pretre (an old priest)—someone who doesn't know when to stop and thinks he's an auteur. So, if you care to, come enter my life and let me tell you about some of the people and instances where my path and that of some special people crossed as we walked together. It has been a great life, I've met some wonderful people who have given me love and who have let me give them my own love. They have given me so much, much more than I deserve, and continue to do so, and that's part of God's gift.

# STORY 1: TURNED UPSIDE DOWN

Coming from a small town as I did, from New Roads, made my experience in the wider world quite limited. With a Cajun background, my first day at the Seminary was a swirling around of the unfamiliar: new people, new classes, new directions and a rigid regimen to follow, led by people about whom I had no idea. But I was favorably impressed by the monks who welcomed me into this new arena: the St. Joseph seminary at St. Ben's.

One thing was certain—I was where I wanted to be, even if my quest was to determine whether being a priest was the right direction of the life I was beginning to try to pursue.

There were surprising realities which I acknowledged at 16 years old—I had never been to a doctor, a barber, or a dentist before I busied myself with the required preparations. The spiritual aspects of my life had been quietly coached by trusted people and their counsel, of which the Sisters were the strongest and most frequent. I was seldom encouraged by the distant Dutch priest in my home town.

Up to that time, before and after World War II, St. Mary Parish had never had an American priest—the Dutch and the French and their missionary care were the usual pastors. But the period in 1942 between Fr. Hoes and Fr. Janssens brought a new reality—the temporary pastor, Fr. Charlie Plauche, a Cajun and very much an American. He arrived but then only for a period of 6 months in the interim. His arrival, coupled with the family cousins who were priests, underlined what quite earlier seemed to be only my childlike inquiry—what to expect after my high school graduation.

That glimpse and Fr. Plauche was all it took—the sprouting seed of possibility opened up. Perhaps, after all, it might be possible that this could be my goal. This new priest (to me) looked like he enjoyed what he was and did. Who knows? And after 4 years, the idea never left, even with the myriad experiences of high school. I felt that the growing gifts I experienced from friends and family helped me to prepare for life.

Once I was accepted into the seminary, with my classes and classmates, the surprise was that I liked it, and, the more time went by, the more I became convinced that this was the life for me—to bring the word of God, the Sacraments, and all that a priest is invested in. And so it has been not only for the 8 years in the seminary curriculum and the fullness of life involved therein, but the 54 years since then.

The surprise was that the Bishop's placing his hands on the heads of the men who ascended the altar as Deacons and returned to their places as Priests of God was for me a tour de force. Could it be true and real?

Of course, and, with my continuing daily decision to live this life fully, to reflect back on the progress of this decision and the many, many people who have touched me with their faith, their optimism, and their investment proved for me the validity of this decision. More than validity is the "giftedness" of what my life has been to me, to my family, and to the people I have dedicated myself to serve.

In Mark's Gospel, we have these words to follow—"For the Son of Man has come not to be served, but to serve and to give his life as a ransom for many." To follow in the footsteps of the Son of Man in this direction is the privilege for me and for others who seek to follow the Good Shepherd, as priests, as deacons, and as the flock of Jesus Christ.

## STORY 2: MOM AND HER CAR

How to talk about an 87-year-old widow, living alone, who was spunky, holy, humorous, independent, and sometimes hilarious? I would like to recall an incident about Mom when we had all these qualities exhibited for us.

## "Lemme Tell You a Story"

Once day, my brothers called to tell me that we, the family, had to decide something about Mom and the signs of her aging. It seemed that the dents and scrapes on her car gave rise to suspicion that Mom's reflexes, and perhaps her vision, called for action by us. Daily she drove the few miles to early morning Mass at St. Mary's, made visits to the Adoration Chapel, brought Holy Communion to the home-bound, did laundering of the Altar Linens, and folded the Church Bulletins, Her daily routine led my brothers, who observed her so closely, to begin to ask some hard questions.

And the whole matter came to a head one day at dinner when the brothers suggested to Mom that perhaps she should have someone else drive her to her many destinations relating to St. Mary's where she was so well-known and loved. The reaction from this suggestion? Explosion!

"What? You're going to take my car away from me? They gave me a license! No way! Look, I taught all of you to walk! I taught all of you to swim! I taught all of you to drive (and in an old stick-shift truck)! And now you're telling me that I can't drive anymore? Oh, no—I want to see who's going to take my keys away from me. It's my car—I paid for it—and I decide what's going to happen here!" Groan.

So, my brothers called in the cavalry, the eldest, the priest, the far-away brother, to bring in the strong force to counter this not unexpected reaction to what was a sensible solution to many questions, fears, and careful maneuvering by the family. So, I got all my priestly equipment ready to diplomatically defuse Mom's opposition—helmet, coat of mail, bullet-proof vest, Roman collar, suit, and even black prayer book to try to bring light to a darkened situation.

Several days after that phone call, I arrived at home to find Mom in the kitchen, as usual, making a fresh pot of coffee for our customary loving and warm conversation and discussion of her and my daily triumphs, failures, and frustrations. I knew that she had noticed my choice of clerical rather than regular casual clothes; fewer jokes: maybe a little stiffness in my greeting her.

After getting my coffee, she and I sat down, and she poured it all out. "I'm sure that you've heard about what the boys are telling me. I think that I shook them up—but they want me to stop driving myself and have someone else drive me to all the things that I do at church. I've thought about it, prayed about it, and I think that I'm going to give my car to Mitzi, my granddaughter. She needs a car, and I think it'll help her, chere petite." Boom! (All the wind gets out of the sails—Holy Spirit, you've done it again!)

But that's not the end of the story. The car was given to Mitzi who came to pick it up. I thought that was all to it, but days later, Mom called to tell me with much emphasis, "Do you know that I gave my car to Mitzi, and, when she came to pick it up, I didn't even get a 'thank you' from that kid? Gratitude? No-o-o." So I got on the phone to that niece who lived a distance from Mom to apprise her of all the dimensions of that exchange.

I unloaded on Mitzi (18 years old at the time). "I don't think you realize what that gift of her car meant to Mom! She was giving you her independence, her freedom, her ability to get around to help all the people whose lives she touches daily. And you didn't even have the grace to thank her!"

Well, it seemed to have done the trick—Mom called me later on to tell me, "I'm sure you didn't have anything to do with that, but boy, Mitzi sent me a thank you card; she sent me a long letter telling me how much she appreciated my car; how nice it was to drive; and how I am such a great grandma, etc., etc." Interesting.

Now, seven years after Mom's death and forty-three years after Daddy's death, I thank God and can only appreciate this "valiant woman" of Scripture and how much in touch with real life she was. Any experience with her has filled me and so many others with such fond memories of how she grappled with life with such zest, humor, and spunk.

# STORY 3: MY DAD: A SURPRISING ENCOUNTER

There were very few things in his life that gave my Daddy fear. Married in 1928, he and Mom lived thru many "Greats"—1927 Great Flood, the Great Depression in 1929, the Great Hurricane of 1935. By 1932, he and Mom had two children and then in 1935 would spend the Hurricane on the streets of New Roads with two mules and a wagon-load of corn to be delivered to the mill. He began as a farmer and moved up to be a self-taught blacksmith; he then became the first welder in town, building his own shop in which his sons and their sons worked in a good business which they would in time carry on.

He loved to hunt and fish; he knew the beauty of nature and taught his family to appreciate the independence he and Mom exhibited. But he also knew well the dangers which that might present. My tale is one of our many family stories, many times told and enjoyed in our after-dinner sessions together at home.

One morning, Daddy had been called out to do some welding in town. His shop was on the outskirts, and, when he returned with the Shop Truck, he drove into the yard and its ruts. Slowly he drove toward the back part of the lot. And then something strange happened—the truck door flew open, and Daddy jumped out of the truck as it slowly continued to roll toward the back fence, the engine still running. He yelled something about "Get my gun! Snake!" My brother exclaimed, "What is that all about?" as Daddy ran swiftly past him toward the office to get something.

From there, Daddy ran back to the truck and its open door, and we heard 3 shots, and then quiet. The truck's engine stopped, and then Daddy in triumph brought out a dead 3 foot garden snake from the ceiling of the truck. Any explanation would have sufficed.

It seems that as Daddy entered the shop yard, this snake, which was in the truck upholstery ceiling, fell and landed in his lap. Daddy's reaction? "I don't care if it's a boat, a car, or my truck. If a snake surprises me, he can have anything I'm in—I'm out of there!"

And what about the gunshots? Without any care, he shot the snake through the upholstery and the roof of the truck.

"Well, how will I fix that up and still have my pride?" was Daddy's concluding question. So, for years after that incident, the Shop Truck (with its bottles of oxygen/acetylene, and its welding machine and tools) was not taken out during a rain for the simple reason that there were 3 bullet holes now added to the roof. Every time that story is told, there is much laughter. He was only surprised, but not afraid!

Daddy's pride was preserved, and another story was added to a colorful life by my Father.

## STORY 4: JIMMY NAVIS— GUILT WITHOUT FAULT

I had been pastor of Our Lady of Lourdes Church, with its 4 Missions, for over a year, and all our parish programs were in full gallop. My Associate, Fr. Benny, and our 3 EMD Sisters were a good team, and things were looking good.

One morning, in early spring, 1966, I was ringing the church bell for 6:30 am Mass, and one of the Sisters came up to me and informed me that there was something lying on the road,

St. Bernard Highway which passed in front of the church. It was and is a very busy thoroughfare at that time in the morning.

Leaving the church, I ran over and saw what was, very evidently, a human body about 200 feet from the church. Running back, I called to a man nearby to get a blanket or sheet to cover the body and flag down motorists as they sped to work. I didn't realize at the time that this man was the driver whose motorcycle, lying on the highway had struck the youngster now bleeding to death on the highway.

I went over to the boy, knelt and gave him absolution, and then I recognized that this boy was Jimmy Navis, the 14-year-old altar boy who lived across the highway from the church and was due to serve the 6:30 Mass. Late, he was rushing on his way to the church from his house when he fell and was struck. Only then did I hear his mother scream when she saw the crowd gathering and realized what had happened. This was possibly the most severe depth of pain I have ever experienced in my priesthood. I knew Jimmy well, loved him and his family, and this touched me deeply.

I had frequently been on him to be on time. He was a good boy, but a little slow, and this morning it cost him his life: he was rushing to go serve at church: and when he got to that busy traffic, he fell, and the motorcycle clipped the top of his head. For years, I would look back at this situation and, although without fault, I felt responsible and guilty. An example of guilt without culpability, but productive of so much suffering.

I had Jimmy's funeral in that church several days later in a sort of daze, of grief, guilt, and need for consolation. This was given to me by my family and the parish family who understood my pain. Now, over 40 years later, I recall this young man with much love, regret, and resolution not to be too hard on those who attempt to help me and us, and whose way of living is to be patiently tolerated.

A sequel to this happening: several years later, Jimmy's only younger brother moved with the family to Texas where he entered the seminary and was ordained a priest, an Oblate of Mary Immaculate. An example of God's inscrutability and our struggles with understanding the events of our lives, and how ambiguous something can be for us mortals as we struggle with God's will.

## STORY 5: VESTIGES OF THE PAST— MY CASSOCK

Only occasionally do I get back into my closet and see my old friends, my once almost second-skin: my cassocks. There are now 2 of them—one older one in black, 41 years old, and the other, Monsignor purple (red cuffs and buttons, many pockets: fru-fru)—21 years old. They stand there on the back part of the rack, waiting.

How times have brought about so many changes in attitude, in daily living. Back in 1946, while preparing for the seminary, I tried out the new cassock made at home by Mom (don't tell her, but it didn't fit very well, only well enough!), and I stood looking at myself in the mirror, with a white cardboard collar, and wondered if I looked like a seminarian, or even a priest!. I actually looked forward to wearing it. And wear it I did—morning, noon, and night—clean, sweaty, and sometimes not so clean.

Came ordination time, the cassocks were new ones made for the occasion by professional tailors and having two pockets and a collar with rabat. O every day, we seminarians wore them—only a T-shirt underneath, black pants, shoes and socks. Summer, winter and fall. It was really our uniform, much like the Army and its dress code. My pastor Bishop Caillouet said, "Father, when you come downstairs, you are a priest, and you dress like a priest—cassock, or suit and Roman collar!"

(Even when riding a bike through City Park—it sounded like being dressed in Paris or Rome).

As I look back from my almost-80 years old and 55 years as a priest, I am brought back by the changes which have occurred. Today, things are much more casual—we are not spooked by dress codes—black pants and shoes, yes. People here know who we are—neat, yes; clean, yes. But coat and collar? Only on special occasions. Why do I have to always dress like a priest? One day, walking thru the Quarter to the Cathedral with black suit and Roman collar, I was pinned to the wall by a drunk who saw me and yelled to me, "Hey, Father, don't play with little boys, you hear?" The urge to kill is not far away, but I kept on walking without looking back.

I think that, today, our feelings run to the same vein as the nuns who also have adopted lay clothes instead of their habits. They do not need a uniform; in fact, they perform their ministry better when they don't wear a sign identifying them. (I can recall that, years ago, some nuns wore their veils only to get a free ride on the streetcar!) We are not some suit of clothes doing for people. We are people, not automatons! This identification can be good or not so good in some circumstances. It's too rigid, uncomfortable, sometimes not appropriate, or even dehumanizing to the priest, and intimidating to some other folks. When you think about it, Bishop Caillouet and his rules are a throw-back!

One of the "cassock memories" is that of my return to the rectory at St. Joseph's in Chauvin after a wedding rehearsal in church one evening in January. My Associate was at a basketball game at the time. As I passed the floor furnace over which I stood that January evening, I smelled smoke and saw it coming up out of the floor furnace. Fire!

The first thing I did was remove my cassock and throw it on the stairs as I raced to call the fire department. Going outside, I went around the side of the raised house to look at the beams beneath the office and saw that the wires attached to the beams were aflame. In 2 hours that fourplex cypress 50-year-old homey rectory was completely gutted, and, with it, everything I and my Assistant owned.

After buying more clothes, we salvaged very little. Fortunately our church records of baptisms, weddings, and funerals were in a fireproof safe which survived. Nothing else was saved. The church, only 20 feet from the rectory, was untouched by the fire.

Today, as I look at those two cassocks in the closet, I don't miss them. They represent legalism and entitlements; however, they sometimes fail to provide us priests and pastors with much more satisfaction in our human and humane relationships with the people we serve. I don't feel that I live in some rarefied air untouched by the cares and concerns of our people—I am part of them. This is what our Lord intended and which the prophet Ezechiel had in mind when he railed, "O you shepherds who pasture themselves and do not pasture my people, my sheep. You wear their wool; you eat their fatlings, but you do not shepherd them. I will come after you," says the Lord.

On a regular basis, I reflect upon these words and search my conscience. The cassock and its strictures represent so much to me bringing our struggles with the Latin language, the canon law, and another era back then. We look for an attitude of service and not of privilege, entitlement, or fear to become our daily mantra. These cassocks are best left where they are so that we can reach our people more readily to serve them as Jesus did and not just be served by them.

## STORY 6: DIFFERENT INTRO TO VIOLET

It was 1957. Ordained 3 years before, I was being introduced to my new assignment as an Assistant Pastor in Our Lady of Lourdes Parish in Violet by my predecessor, Fr. Hubert Brou.

We met at the rectory, and I took my boat and motor with Hubert to the "Fort." The Merrill Perez family for many years had leased this 3-story brick structure situated 1,000 yds in Lake Borgne. There they fished, trawled, skied, sailed and crabbed on holidays and weekends. A very good Catholic family, they had a beautiful place for their families and children to spend time together, which they did every weekend and holidays.

This day was a holiday, and Hubert arranged for me to go out with him to meet the family. It was a lovely day to be out on the lake. I arrived around 11:am, and we drove the boat to the wharf out on the water. I noticed as we neared the wharf that two men were there waiting for us, while the rest of the family was trawling, or in the fort itself.

When I got to the wharf, one of the men took the rope and tied us up; Hubert got out and turned. As I climbed up, he said, "Fr. Roy, I want you to meet some great friends: Rabbit and Tookie; they are brothers-in-law. This is your new assistant, Fr. Roy." I put out my hand.

Instead of taking my hand, with smiles on their faces, Rabbit and Tookie came to me, one on each side. They each took an arm and said, "Father, welcome to Our Lady of Lourdes and to Violet" and promptly threw me off the wharf into the water: wallet, shoes, clothes, all without any regard to how I liked it or cared. This was the first of many experiences of that kind.

Well, I don't know if they knew or cared how I would take that treatment—I was so surprised; it was so unexpected—my mouth wide open, spitting up water. After all, I'm a priest, and they should treat me with respect. But, as a good priest, I climbed back on the wharf, and soon they, too, were off the wharf into the water, clothes and all. A good beginning.

That family was so good to me for the 4 years I ministered there with the EMD Sisters—I ate many great meals with them; they heard my groans about the crotchety old pastor and his antics. They loved him but understood that his life had been a difficult one. He was there for 23 years, and they understood his poverty, bordering on rudeness. But also they continued to be nice to him although he didn't respond with any kind of grace. This would change toward them and toward me in time as it would with the Sisters.

It really took the Sisters to bring this about—Sr. Paula and Sr. Aquinas would arrive to live in the parish 3 months later. They and I underwent the pastor's rudeness, impoliteness, and brooding scrutiny for several years before he began to trust us and believe that we loved him.

Before we ended our stay and ministry in the parish with its 5 churches, we became fast friends of Fr. Schneider (in fact, he asked me to preach at 5 of his 50th jubilee Masses, and I was an honored pall-bearer at his funeral years later). I learned to appreciate and admire his zeal and dedication in difficult circumstances, although I also learned not to expect much gentleness.

He had been a soldier in the German army and was shot at by the American Army in WWI. He became one of the prime movers for the formation of the Washington Artillery unit in the American Army after he was in the US for several years. He loved a soldier's life.

Later on, his heart was to be broken when his unit was sent overseas, and he was refused to move with them because of accusations of being a Nazi by people in the parish. In spite of that, he remained in the Army, to retire 20 years later, even getting over his bitterness about the unfairness of the people whose identity he knew. He became a political force in St. Bernard parish—he was consulted by all the politicians on both sides of the issues which came up.

I myself learned to listen to him as he shared his wisdom and experience in the parish. Later on, with Hurricane Betsy in

1965, 3 of our chapels would be destroyed by the wind and the water of the Storm, and San Pedro Pescador was built to replace them. In 2005, this church, too, would be flooded by Hurricane Katrina, 12 feet off the ground, and flooded with 6 feet of water over its upstairs floor.

We are all grateful that Fr. Schneider never saw this devastation when all of St. Bernard would be assaulted by this flood; it would have drawn bitter tears from him. May he rest in peace.

## STORY 7: A JOYFUL DAY AT ORDINATION

Seminary life both St. Ben's (the minor seminary) and at Notre Dame (the graduate theology school) were quite agreeable to me. After having graduated from high school in 1946, I entered and was thrust into some great friendships and fascinating study.

The preparation for priesthood was rather arduous and regimented—we were continually dressed in black cassocks, white collars, and white surplices for the liturgy. It was only when we were in recreation and sports that we were dressed in anything else. We had the rule of silence; we lived by the bell; our classes were in Latin mostly; we carried many academic hours; but largely, it was a strict not a bad life. Seminary for me would last eight years.

In our final year or so, we were ordained Subdeacons: a step away from the priesthood. As Subdeacons, we took the vow of celibacy, an oath of obedience to our church superiors, and a promise of "praying for the church, with the Liturgy of the Hours" (also in Latin). But a good life, really.

As we got closer to ordination to priesthood, we had a retreat held on the seminary grounds. In those days we were not allowed to leave the seminary grounds without permission.

We had no cars, or radios, or air-conditioning in our rooms: television would come later, after ordination when we were assigned to parishes as priests.

Ferried by busses to St. Louis Cathedral for ordination, we were dressed in our new cassocks and carried our vestments and books. During the ceremony, the twelve of us in my class climbed to the altar step as seminarians, we had the bishop impose his hands on us in ordination, and we then returned to our places in the sanctuary as priests of God. A very moving moment.

After that, we again faced the bishop. As we each offered our folded hands to him, he covered them and asked us, in Latin, "Do you promise me and my successors obedience and respect?" Our response, "Libenter (freely)!" This brought from each of us the silent prayer, "Please O Lord, let me not have to regret what I am doing now!"

After giving our early blessings to those who were now our fellow-priests and to the congregation, we unvested and moved out of the Cathedral. It was thrilling: we were facing assignments to parishes in the archdiocese where we would then begin to live independently from our families for the rest of our lives. This "break" would touch us deeply with the thought of "It's for the Lord and for the Church!" My mother would reflect on this when asked about her son who was now a priest. She would respond, "He is no longer my son—I've given him to the Blessed Mother."

After the ceremony, we were allowed to return to the seminary with our parents on our own. However, there was a luncheon in the seminary dining room for our fathers (but without our mothers!—a strange arrangement). But that was okay: we seldom questioned these orders—obedience sometimes was truly blind! Walking down Pere Antoine Alley after the ordination and blessing, my dad, mom, and I had a chance to speak as we headed toward Notre Dame. I didn't know what thoughts were going through my parents' minds and hearts. As we left the cathedral alley, we stopped walking, and my dad told me something that made it all so worthwhile. He said, "My boy, today, for the second time in your life, you have made us very happy—first, the day you were born, and this day when you were ordained a priest."

Other memories began to crowd in of places, people, and situations which make up this great life—some so funny, some so serious—and all parts of God's unfolding goodness manifested and "unrolled" for us to spread out on our blankets to prize, reflect upon, to question in time, and to value.

As the priest-poet Lacordaire once wrote, "To touch the Body of Christ, to bring the Christ to his people: this is your life, O priest of Jesus Christ."

## STORY 8: STORMS A-PLENTY

In our area and in my lifetime, there have been many storms: 1935, 1947 (Flossie), Betsy in '65, Camille '69, and then Katrina. I have not been really fearful of storms (perhaps not enough), but now they do cause some caution.

When it was certain that Katrina was headed our way, NOAA and the Weather Channel urged us to move, after the city officials began telling us to move. So I did, with Sr. Janie Quatman and Sr. Paula who live in Houma (Jane the Super-Nurse at Terrebonne General and Paula at Annunziata for many years). We evacuated to Baton Rouge until the Storm passed, and then, knowing that New Orleans had had such a flood and we would not return for a long time, we went to New Roads to my brother Jerry and Adley's. There I worked in 3 different shelters for 3 weeks.

Once it became clear that I could return, I brought Sr. Paula back to their home in Houma and headed back to Holy Spirit.

There I found no lights, no birds, few people and much fear of looting. Dismal time. Broken trees, mounds of debris, all the detritus of a bad storm to affect our State and City for many years. Bad enough that in the early days of another storm, the fear begins as we track the circling cyclone on the Weather Channel.

When I returned to Holy Spirit, I began to put things back together. Fran Laudun, our Custodian, and Brother Terry Todd from the Jesuits next door did not evacuate, so they kept our place in good shape. We had power and telephones by that time. I got a call from the Insurance Office at the Archdiocese of N.O. that they would send inspectors to take stock and photos of our facilities.

When they arrived, there were 3 of them, with cameras and tape-measures. They checked all our buildings and took pictures (we needed a new roof over all our buildings, and we had a hole poked in our garage roof). Finishing, they asked me if we had anything else for them to look at. And I told them that I had seen the ceiling in our upstairs classrooms which showed that we had had bad leaks there—they needed to look at it and photograph it.

So the 4 of us entered the elevator. It began as usual and, quite soon, came to a lurching stop. Grunts. What to do now? Push the buttons. Nothing. Push again—still nothing. Use the elevator phone—dead. How about our cell phones (all 4 of them)—deadness.

Remember now: no one knew we were there—and it was over 100 degrees in there! I prayed—they prayed silently. Then, after a half hour, we began looking at the ceiling of the elevator to perhaps use a trap-door to escape. And me with my replaced knees. Not much hope.

About that time, I remember saying, "Please, Jesus, get us out of here!" Again we tried the buttons, the phones, and still nothing. Then I heard the older man of the group push at the door (no handles) and exclaim, "God damn it—Open this door!" And it opened! You have never seen 4 men move as fast as we did to get out of there.

Once we were out, I told that man, "You know, I've seen prayers answered quickly before, but never this fast! You're amazing!" He only hung his head.

That's not the end of the story. They finished their business and left. I had gotten so warm in that elevator that I cooled off too fast, and, in the next day or so, I caught pneumonia.

I evacuated for hurricane Rita again to Houma where I stayed to get well. Sr. Janie and Sr. Paula nursed me in their house during the fears of Rita—wild dreams of having to "get out—the water's coming up." Watching the ceiling of their house, we made sure that, if we flooded, we would be able to climb into the attic, or, if we had to, we could stay at the room at the hospital, courtesy of Sr. Janie and her key and position at Terrebonne General. But thank God, no need—we didn't even lose our power. What relief. Days later, I returned home, grateful.

There was more storm-stuff—Gustav, Ike and their damage to Texas and the Louisiana coast. We again evacuated to Baton Rouge and again experienced the fears, heat, boredom, angers, impatience, but also the generosity and ingenuity of Sr. Paula's family members who did for Guy Leblanc, her sister, for her, me and Sr. Janie, and got us through. God bless them; next time, who knows what will happen?

## STORY 9: OUR "NEW HARD TIMES"

Recently, Time Magazine described the panic of Wall Street and its fears in a cover story, with photo, of the "2008 Black Friday." We saw a new version of bread lines and soup kitchens as people joined the unemployment ranks. And it brought me back to my childhood 1942 or thereabouts and our own privations. Not food stamps or commodities, but an outdoor privy, coal-oil lamps, and exposure to a measure of poverty. Without realizing it, we were in Hard Times. Our family was composed of Daddy, Mom, and me, the oldest of 3 sons, Pat would come later, in 1945.

Uncle Horace and Aunt Nannan had 2 children. An unemployed carpenter, he moved from Hamburg to "La Ville" to find work and did find it there. They first lived on Jeanette Street in New Orleans and later moved to Zimple. He found work at Delta Shipyard, where the welding trade he learned in Daddy's shop enabled him to get a job.

We had been close to them and went to visit them one weekend in a one-seat Dodge coupe. Behind the car seat was a trap-door thru which one could go in and out of the trunk space without having to stop the car or open the trunk. Kearn was a baby, so Jerry and I had to share that darkness and close quarters for the l-o-o-n-g ride to the City. Regularly, Daddy had to hear, "Daddy, Jerry's touching me!" Or, "Shut up, you, that's my song. Find your own, Maudi," we whispered to each other—boys: "Big brother, ha, ha ha."

When we finally arrived (after being in the darkness for what seemed like days), we were warmly greeted. The prospects: swimming in that beautiful pool at Audubon Park only a few blocks away, riding bikes around the city, and meeting with Roy Lemoine and Dotty. Roy loved to ride his bike early in the morning, and sometimes we saw the milkman deliver milk in bottles and also deliver doughnuts on the front steps. How delicious: he wouldn't buy them of course. Also, Aunt Nannan was a great cook—she would buy bread dough and make flapjacks, fritters, and beignets, which we all loved.

One day, we decided to ride bikes to Ponchartrain Beach, a long way. I borrowed Bobby's bike, and with Roy we set out. (Today, it's really a long way, but then, even further). As we neared the Beach, we stopped on an overpass to look ahead and rest. While we waited, a policeman drove up to speak with us in our fears. "Hello, boys. Where you from? What are you doing? Are those your bikes—do you have a license for them?" "Oh, Oh, this is Bobby's bike. No, he doesn't seem to have a license—are you supposed to have one? I didn't know that. I'm sorry; we're from the country."

"Now git away from here. If I catch you kids around here again, I'm gonna take your bikes and maybe put you in jail!" The promise of the fun at the Beach was dimmed.

So, getting away, we rode our bikes as fast as we could and then hid them in the bushes not to lose them, and got on the midway. I was scared to be on foot, but we had fun coming, so it was okay.

We spent a couple of hours at the Beach—the rides we couldn't afford and the food which smelled so good were not for us to do without. But we drank water (yuck! It tasted like the chlorine in the pool water!) Then we rode back home, always looking out for another policeman (Le Sheriff) who would ask for another license, which we didn't have.

We were poor, but we didn't know it. As Mom has said so often, "Eh bein, we didn't know any better." The fun we had, and we had fun, was simple—we sang, we played together with our cousins and their people, and we had a grand time.

The trip back was another experience of darkness and waiting: "Daddy, are we there yet? How much longer?" "Quiet back there—say the Rosary, and don't let me hear you fighting each other again." Hours later, we finally were home again in New Roads and could get out of that cave. It was good to be back home again to St. Jude street and our regular existence.

# STORY 10: MOM'S REVENGE

Let me tell you about my Mom and her act of revenge. Well into her 80's, she began to do more craft projects with the Council on Aging in New Roads. She decided to crochet a couple of wall hangings for Ms. Thelma's kitchen.

So, she got on her 3-wheel bicycle and pedaled to the National Food Store about a mile from home where she first went in and bought 2 saucers. Then, leaving them in the basket on her bike, (unlocked of course) she went next door to the TG&Y store for the thread, the cherry and strawberry decals, and the wall hooks. Coming out from that store, she came back to the bike, and she found that her saucers had been stolen! The audacity, the cupidity of that crook!

She went back in again to re-buy her things and carried all purchases in her arms to make sure they were secure against any thief. Getting back on her bike (which had not been stolen), she headed home. What to do? She pondered that problem as she pedaled back home. "Ah yes, I got it—I know how I'll fix that "Fils de putaine; enfant de garce!"

Arriving home, she parked her bike in the garage and went inside to find a shoe box with tissue paper inside it. Then she went into the back yard with a small shovel where she went to some of the "Gravy Train offerings" of her dog Sandy on the ground and put them into the tissue papered box. "Ha, Ha, Ha! What a great idea to get him back for stealing my stuff." Then, she wrapped the box with a lovely ribbon and even put a bow on it.

Getting back on her bike, she pedaled back to the same store with the gift-wrapped box in her basket, gloating and laughing all the way. When she got back to the store, she parked her bike in the same spot as before. She left the "present" in the basket in full view and re-entered the store where she walked all the way to the back of the store. (She didn't want "him" to see her.)

After a while, she returned to the bike, and sure enough, the present was gone! O how sweet it was! "I got him—he's mine—another gotcha." And then she headed for home, pedaling with joy and exultation. "O boy, I can't wait to tell this to my boys. They're going to enjoy this so much. I fixed that son of a gun—got him good. Imagine what it will be like when he opens that gift-wrapped box and only finds some of my 'Sandy-poop!'"

And then, realization set in. She stopped pedaling when the coming guilt came into view.

"I can't tell that to my boys. They're all going to think I'm nasty, that this was dirty! No, I can't do it." And so the silence of several years set in until finally, years later, she revealed to me her secret.

"Was that being nasty, mon cher? He didn't have the right to steal from me. I know you'll tell me the truth and not tease me." All to an explosion of laughter. Naturally, it didn't stop there—soon, the entire family wanted to give her a medal because of her cleverness and the supreme "Gotcha!" she had accomplished.

Incidentally, she never tried to make such a craft project again. Instead, she had to endure the loving teasing of her family, but still she told me in private she had to chuckle every time she thought about it.

She never found out who had done this to her, and she didn't want to know. But she could exult over "getting him, and getting him good, le Maudi."

# STORY 11: A BOY AND HIS DOG

It was 1942. I was 12 and had a romantic offer from the folks next door. If I would bring Puddy Griffin to a dance, she would give me a male puppy from the litter that her dog had delivered. O, I wanted him—an "all American dog"—no blood-lines, a midsize rat terrier, a friendly dog. And our family did not have one.

So, I made arrangements for Daddy to bring Puddy and me to the dance at the Woodmen of the World hall in New Roads. There was nothing much to say about that (I didn't know how to dance and didn't much care about learning. I would have preferred to play in the band at the dance instead, but it was an agreement.) We went, and then came home, and I got my dog!

He was about half a year old, and I loved him—his name was "Callou"—that didn't mean much, but he was my dog, and I loved him. He was smart and beautiful. Callou and I played together, he and I and my 2 brothers—sometimes he would retrieve, but mostly we were "podners"—he was mine. I groomed him, bathed him, had my name on his collar, and we went places together.

After I had had Callou a couple of years, he grew to full size. One day, after I had walked home from school (it was in the fall), we were in Mr. Pourciau's field picking pecans. I hadn't seen Callou since I had left for school that morning, but we were busy, and I didn't think much about it.

We had been picking for a while when Mr. Brieyard, who lived on the main street into town, came up and called to me. This was unusual—he didn't come around much except to ask about mowing his lawn. As he approached, I somehow had misgivings. He called me over and said to me, "Jay, I think it's your dog that's lying in the ditch on Main Street near my house. He was hit by a car this morning: he's not dead yet, but he's bad off and is still moaning. He won't live."

I ran the three blocks to the place by myself and got to the vacant lot near where poor Callou was lying. It was ugly; he was still moaning. I was heartbroken, but more than that, I felt his pain. Leaving him, I went back home and got a shovel and my 410 shotgun and one shell, and came back. First I dug his grave, and then did what I'm sure was one of the most difficult things I've ever done: I aimed the gun at his head and pulled the trigger. He made no sound; I did, and then rolled him into the grave and covered him, while praying for him and thanking God for the joy he had given me with poor Callou.

Daddy, when I told him about it all, praised me for what I had done in putting Callou out of his misery, and he told me, "Well, you know that's the danger when you have a dog who can run loose. Maybe you should have seen to it when you left for school that he couldn't run into the street and get run over. Maybe if you want, we can find you another dog."

By that time I didn't want another dog; besides, my brother Jerry had one, and that seemed to be enough for us.

I have never forgotten that incident. O yes, I've had dogs given to me—years later, a registered Cocker spaniel was given to me as I was moving from Chauvin to NO, which I gave to my other brother, but he didn't take care of it, and it died. Another time, someone gave me a Brittany Spaniel, which was a beautiful dog, when I lived a couple of blocks from where we would build our church, and that one I gave to a nephew. Unfortunately that one, too, didn't last. The French Poodle given to me for Mom jumped the fence, and it, too, was hit by a car. No more.

Now, years later, I think back on Callou and his place in my young life. I still don't have a dog—I've seen too many pastors whose animals ran their parishes. I've learned to prize my solitude when I can have it.

But honestly, I suspect that Callou decided that I wouldn't go thru that once again. We've had dogs at home, and still have; they have given us some great memories—a string of Cocker-spaniels who were part of the family and loved by us all. But never MY DOG. And that's a place in my life which I can live with—I love pets, especially dogs, but never cats, or birds, or goldfish, and at my age I am satisfied with my life and my ministry. Callou was a gift that I prized, and I'm grateful that he was mine for the joy he gave me.

## STORY 12: WHAT GOES AROUND COMES AROUND

My dad was quite a man—smart, interested, and interesting. He was a blacksmith-turned-welder; great husband and father; he loved to fish, to hunt, to shoot (even to shooting a camera: he even built his own darkroom to develop his own photos). He had only a 3$^{rd}$ grade education, but he educated himself (with Mom and her 5$^{th}$ grade schooling). From Mansura, he had little advantages other than those he made himself. He was a very strong man. But he still smoked (although only rolling his own, which kept the number of cigarettes down).

It was 1962, and Dad had been skeet-shooting the day before. He had supper that Sunday night, went to bed, and fell asleep. About 4:30 the next morning, Mom said that he got up to use the bathroom and returned to bed. She went back to sleep and, all of a sudden, heard him snoring in a way he never had before. She called him and realized that it was not snoring but the death-rattle. She screamed. My youngest brother, still living in the front room, ran up and then took his keys to go into the shop next-door to get oxygen to try to revive him.

## "Lemme Tell You a Story"

Next door to Mom's house, Howard and Rosemary Smith heard her scream, and Howard came over to help. When he saw Dad's condition, he began CPR, even to mouth-to-mouth resuscitation. But all to no avail—Dad was probably dead when Mom first noticed: a massive coronary. Howard continued the CPR and mouth-to-mouth until Fr. Lefebvre arrived to anoint Dad. It all happened so quickly, Mom recalled.

Dad had seldom been sick; in fact, he could suffer silently without anyone knowing it—never a complaint about any condition in himself or in his surroundings. He was liked by everyone in New Roads, black and white, young and old, and was known around town as a very outgoing someone who talked a lot. But in the family, we all felt that he said very little about himself or his concerns, and I still think that was so.

At any rate, for 40 years later, Mom lived the life of a widow, and in her "church doings" was quite involved. She had begun to bring the Eucharist to the homebound whenever anyone was sick and asked for it. She took great pride in doing that, considering (what it really is) that this was a privilege. She was good at it with her ability to pray with great faith.

One Saturday afternoon, Mom was asked by Rosemary Smith, next door, to bring Howard Holy Communion because he was sick with the flu. She agreed and set a time when she would come, after bringing the Eucharist to several sick people. Howard was the last one on her list.

When she got to Howard's, Rosemary told her that Howard was in the back yard in his pajamas and would return. As he re-entered the house, Mom began the prayers as Howard returned to bed. After giving him Holy Communion, she said the prayers and, looking at Howard, told him, "Howard, cher, you look awful. What's the matter?" And, chilling her, he answered, "I feel awful. I just took poison, Paraguay—a strong herbicide." "How much did you take?" "As much as I could swallow." Howard sold seeds, fertilizers, and weed-killers in his store.

Immediately they called the ambulance; he was brought to the hospital and had his stomach pumped, but in 2 hours, Howard was dead. Bedlam—Mom was stunned and, during his funeral, she couldn't believe this had happened.

Later on, Mom told me about the whole ordeal. And it struck me then, and now, that there we have a good example that God does not sleep (as Mom frequently said). I mean that, as Howard was willing to reach out to help Daddy in his death-struggle, so she was able to reach out to Howard with Holy Communion when he was in his final hours. She felt that she sort of repaid him for his own concern and kindness at a time when she was so needy.

"What goes around comes around" is an old saying. It certainly was operative in our family, and I feel that it is part of our family lore. I am grateful to God and rejoiced with Mom when she told me this story.

## STORY 13: JERRY AND HIS '32 CHEVY

My brother Jerry is only 3 years younger than I. He is smart (smarter than he thinks he is), musical, loyal—and a wonderful mechanic, but also very, very conservative in his outlook and values. "N'import": anyway, he is a great father, husband, grandfather, and great-grandfather.

He loves to tinker with automobiles (once he told me that if he had his druthers, he would have a car junkyard because then he could work on cars to his heart's content). There's no telling what his poor wife, Adley would say; she is such a lady. He knows a value when he sees one—he is the first in our family to get a sailboat which we all had such fun with. He has had at least 5 different businesses which he started and succeeded, but which he abandoned when they interfered with his presence in A.J. Roy's Welding and Machine Shop. He now has owned and run the shop with his children after Dad's death 47 years ago. Today he is more at home at his welding table on a rolling stool than anywhere else in the world.

Somehow or other, Jerry found out about an available 1932 Chevrolet coupe (with rumble seat: I think it was our cousin Richard's). He traded things to get it and fix it. And fix it he did: he was so good at it. He is a superb mechanic (unlike Daddy who didn't like to work on cars: he "only repaired things"). Jerry repainted and tuned it, and all of us rode around with him thru town and in the country. It was a fine car (even though it was almost 30 years old!) He loved to pile a bunch of boys and girls in it and ride around town, over hill and dale. The interesting thing about the Chevy is that it ran better in reverse than it did in forward, but as Mom said, "Eh bien, we didn't know any better. Laisse faire."

At the time, I was in the seminary for several years and was home only in the summer when I experienced all this with the bunch.

An occasion I remember is that Daddy wanted a garden, so he had a truck deliver some good soil for it and piled it up right inside the garden gate. Jerry found a way to drive into the garden, and then he welded a blade to the back bumper of his car. Then he "bulldozed" the dirt around the garden, back and forth, forth and back and, of course, just in reverse!

All of us thought that that was so funny, and yet it did the job. After finishing the garden, Jerry removed the blade from the back bumper and then went on his merry way. He and I had worked with Daddy to build the shop (really, Daddy and Jerry did, because I had to study that summer, jumping 2 grades to be ordained ahead of time). We poured the slab for the new shop floor—2 wheelbarrows, and Daddy ran the cement mixer. That was a hot summer, but we built it, and it was finished before the next winter. Jerry and Daddy had managed to get the needed lumber and build it—a great job.

Except for milking our cows Alice and Jane, I had more to do with studying than with working in the shop. I had my duties as the rest did, Kearn included, but they ran the shop as we built it, and then it was set up to be running so splendidly. Jerry had a hand in everything to do with the shop.

It was a glorious shop which stood for many years until Jerry and Kearn (who was now graduated and working there) decided to replace the wooden building (which was prone to fire) with a steel building twice the size of the original. All of us learned to weld, cut, and burn iron and help the shop along. It was a good experience, but few things gave us as much fun as Jerry's 1932 Chevy.

## STORY 14: PAT—SMELL LIKE CHANEL No. 5

My youngest brother Pat was born in October, 1945. He was the only one of us to be born in a hospital—we lived on St. Jude Street on the eastern end of town. I was a senior in HS, Kearn was still in grammar school, and Jerry was already working in the shop every day with Daddy. I think that Pat's birth was unexpected—Mom was already 41, but he was most welcomed by the family—we gloried in this new baby. He called himself "PtPat-Patroy." (Whenever someone gave me a slice of chewing gum while at band practice, I broke it in half, and saved it for Mom—she loved Juicy Fruit gum, even if it had lost all its sugar from being in my pocket)!

Pat had the world by the tail! We carried him around and played with him; even Sandy our family dog would almost break his tail wagging when Pat was around. And of course he didn't do well in school. He was just not interested much in school and books: he had to be pushed. This is where Kearn worked so hard to get him thru, and did succeed, even if it was from a Brothers' school and their discipline in Alexandria. It was not that he was not intelligent—he was: but he loved the shop and being with Daddy more than school, working with his hands, especially as a machinist, and still does. Machinery comes easily to him.

After he graduated from high school, Pat was in line for the draft. So, instead of waiting, he decided to join the National Guard unit in New Roads. This was near the Berlin Wall occasion—he had to go for Basic Training in Fort Gordon, Georgia. From what I remember, it wasn't too bad for him—he always came out on his feet. Whenever he couldn't figure it out, somehow he lucked out on it. One instance stands out for me.

Pat was courting Jeannette at the time. When he finished Basic, he had a leave at home, and he spent most of his time, at her house, in love—"en grande amour." Even if they were quite young, both of them only 18, they were determined to marry, much to our chagrin. Cautions went nowhere: "Yes, but we're in love!" (That "yes, but" still is his method to get what he's after.) And Jeannette went along with him in this.

When Pat finished his leave, he caught a plane in Baton Rouge to go back to the Army in Georgia. He was exhausted and asked the stewardess on the plane to please wake him when they landed in Atlanta, the nearest city to Fort Gordon. That went okay until, after the plane left Atlanta, he woke up and asked when they would get there. "Sorry, the next landing will be in S. Carolina." So, he waited (and maybe slept again).

Getting off the plane in S. Carolina and still in uniform, Pat brought his duffel bag to the highway and threw out his thumb. Not 10 minutes hitchhiking and a car stopped to pick him up. Not surprisingly (to us), the driver of the car was his sergeant from the next barracks at Fort Gordon who brought him in so that the next morning, Pat was right on time for early formation. Lucky.

This is the way of Pat. If we got into music and records, Pat picked up on our "leavings," which means extra speakers, an unneeded amplifier, or records. He rigged up a speaker system over Mom's only bathroom so that when he was there, the house was rocking and rolling. Oh, he was good in the shop, but he didn't like to get to work on time. He finally left the shop to get a job at Ethyl Corp. in Baton Rouge, a good job, where he stayed for several years.

When Daddy died suddenly in 1962, Pat was sleeping in the front room, and, when he saw what was happening, in his underwear, barefooted, he got his shop keys and ran across the lot to bring, on his shoulder, a heavy oxygen cylinder and mask to revive Daddy. But to no avail—Daddy was already dead.

Today, Pat is a father to Clyde, Mitzi, and Shelly who have given him and Jeannette 4 grandchildren. They love their dogs (I think they have 4 Rottweilers!!!) And Pat operates a crane with a Tree Service which, in view of our hurricanes and their damage, has provided him with a good living, even if he has to work so hard. He lives on the Island, near the "Discharge" canal.

I don't see him as much as I do Jerry and Kearn and their families, but, regularly, I call him on Sunday mornings just to see how he is doing. His health is good. But we all say, "Pat can fall into a cesspool, and, you watch, he'll come out smelling like Chanel No. 5." God bless him.

## STORY 15: KEARN, A STRAIGHT ARROW

If there is any man in our family who was and is a straight arrow, it is Kearn. Intelligent, gentle, sensitive, hard-working, and holy, he is an example to me and to us of someone who is earnestly and generously in pursuit of loving God. He was the son who would have been Mom's daughter, but no regrets—he was a beautiful presence to Mom after Daddy died so young, in 1962.

Kearn has so often mentioned how much he so wished to go to college but couldn't because we couldn't afford it. And yet, when I asked if he would like to pursue the Priesthood, he thought about it seriously. Then he had the courage to tell me that he wanted his own family which made his being a priest a moot question. But he is a great Christian, a loving husband to Jeanie, and also a loving father and grandfather to his family who all worship the ground he walks on.

Of all my brothers, we are the closest—there is nothing Kearn or I would not reveal about ourselves: we have had so many very close conversations together, even if it was on his "Mule" cart in his pecan orchard. We have done this a lot these past years. I depend on his wisdom in much of my ministry. He is serious—he has suffered a great deal in his early life.

Daddy's death was such an unanticipated happening. At the time, Kearn and I were both in the Army (because of the Berlin Crisis and our mobilization in the National Guard—me to a MASH Hospital, and Kearn to a Recon unit). In fact, when Jeanie and Kearn got married, it was in St. Landry Church in Opelousas: I got 4 seminarians to come with me to sing for the wedding. It went off well—all the drive there and back, we talked, sang, and enjoyed being together, without the radio or the news.

So, when I returned to Holy Rosary Church in New Orleans, I went in to my pastor, Bishop Caillouet and greeted him. His response? "Hello, Soldier!" "Whadda ya mean, soldier?" "Well, you're in the Army, and you report to Jackson Barracks in 3 days, and in 3 weeks, Ft. Sill, Oklahoma (!), for there's no telling how long." Oh, oh.

Kearn was able to be on active duty at Ft. Polk only part of that year. He returned home and the shop, and it was during that year that Daddy died. Mom was devastated, and Kearn was there to support and comfort her as did Jerry, Adley (a great deal), and Jeanie.

Also, it would be only a short time afterwards that Jeanie became seriously ill. Kearn went thru the tortures of hell getting her back—and was successful. They have raised a family of 3 boys who are now well-married, with children. Kearn is very active in St. Mary's-Lector, commentator, Eucharistic Minister, Kiwanis Club, even Pastoral Council—I would have loved to have him in my parish!

In one of the episodes of Kearn's life, I saw his skill with music. While still in high school, he got together a group of youngsters to form a band and practiced at Mom's. They were a good band: I still recall with much affection one of the songs they played as a sort of theme: "Charmaine." Kearn fell deeply in love with the piano player—Mary Ellen, who fell in love with him, smart girl.

That romance ended in pain—they broke up for some reason, although he still speaks of her with affection. Last year, while we were at the Marksville casino, Kearn brought a couple up and told me, "Jay, I would like to introduce you to friends of mine: Mary Ellen and her husband." I almost fell out and was so glad to see her again—I had admired her when the band was together.

I speak with Kearn and Jerry a couple of times a week, to keep up with their lives and families. The calls are always welcome, and I enjoy them. We worry about one another and so are open to helping each other. Mom's death, after being "out of it" for a couple of years, was not a cause for pain—she had lived a full, good life and was ready to go back to Daddy in God. We speak of her and Daddy with such nostalgia and joy. God has been so good to us.

These days, Kearn has sold a major part of his land to someone who values and respects what it means to own that land and the pecan trees which Kearn has so lovingly tended. He has agreed to help out in the shop by doing machine work when there is need: he is so good at it and is energetic enough to keep it up. What a good man! He is ready to help in any way that he can and is generous and caring enough to help out as a good friend, brother, and companion. And Kearn is that.

## STORY 16: HURRICANE BETSY STUFF

Betsy arrived in St. Bernard parish on Sept. 9, 1965—it never occurred to us to consider evacuation: the people of St. Bernard had endured many bad storms and were up to remaining in the old courthouse shelter until it all passed. Having endured the winds and rains in the rectory at Our Lady of Lourdes in Violet, early, at 5:00 the next morning, I and my Assistant, Fr. Benny, drove with the 3 EMD sisters to see what we could of the damage and conditions below us.

When we arrived at the Courthouse/school (now a shelter for 1,000 people) there was pandemonium—the shelter manager, who lived further down toward Yscloskey, had tried to get the people evacuated to Chalmette at midnight the night before when the winds switched. When they refused to leave the shelter, he said, "Well, if you won't leave, I'm going home." And did so. So, that flock of people, all related to one another, were left to fend for themselves with a flooded yard and no electricity, water, radio contact, food, or Red Cross help.

Perceiving this, I went in and began to get the cafeteria manager who lived nearby to open up the cafeteria and, if nothing else, make coffee. We went to the hardware store to get some large plastic garbage cans, cleaned them, and then tapped a large cistern next door to get rainwater and brought it to the cafeteria. It was a very dicey situation: no one in command and no contact with the outside world.

Ms. Leona, the cafeteria manager, was very resourceful—she had some food commodities in storage and made that do for the next 2 weeks. I realized that I knew most of those people from having been stationed in the parish for several years, and they would listen to me as I tried to organize the whole business. The bathrooms began quickly to be a problem and there was no sewerage. Water covered the yards around and the people were under mounting stress. They had no idea what their homes had undergone, or whether they had any homes left down below. And they had no way on the single highway to get there—they would need boats to do that, and those boats were all down below.

It took a lot of doing to get some organization. Some of those people were "grabbers"—they took what they wanted without regard for others. I did a lot of desperate praying and swearing until finally, a week later, the Red Cross came in with radios, blankets, cots, and water. My own family in New Roads had no idea (they heard that it was bad), whether I had survived or where I was. They had planned to launch a boat in the Mississippi river to get to me somehow.

One of the instances which made it all even more stressful was that the black school, miles away, had gotten busloads of poor black folks from Plaquemines parish and arranged to get 6 busloads evacuated 10 miles up the road to relieve the crowding in the school/shelter. We arranged to get the busses one night and, after giving them supper, in convoy we drove to a small school in Chalmette where they would stay. We were told that the deputies would open the locked school and get them bedded down.

I went to Our Lady of Prompt Succor in Chalmette, which had sustained no visible damage, to get some votive candles which would provide light for those poor people, and drove back to the school. Just as I got there, the busses came in, and the people emerged in the darkness there. Soon, the sheriff's deputies came in, BUT CARRYING CATTLE PRODS! I was

## "Lemme Tell You a Story"

enraged. I told the head man, "What the hell are you doing with those? Those damned things are for animals, and these are people. You must be some sort of Nazis—take those things away!" The poor people were aged, tired, scared, down and out; one of them was an epileptic and threatened a seizure. When the deputy came back, he told me, "Listen, priest, you're not going to tell my men what to do! I could put you in jail."

I responded, "Okay, you put me in jail and I'll have your job, I promise you, you SOB" (I had never spoken that way before, but it did the trick: I was really bluffing, but no matter). We got the people a large hall in the school and lit the candles, which provided them with some security as they made ready for the night. I then returned to the shelter to the same grief.

The next several days were also very difficult. One day, Nolan asked me if he could borrow my boat and motor from Violet to go to Yscloskey where he had fully loaded his trawler with ice and fuel but was turned back by the storm. He would bring back that ice to take care of the medicine in the crowd. Of course I agreed.

Streaming with sweat, I said Mass in the gym the next morning. I remember the Gospel, "God has visited his people." Very fitting. Afterwards, I had the best drink of ice water of my life—Nolan brought me a tall glass and was that refreshing and life-giving! Days later, help began to arrive—a radio and Red Cross personnel.

One day our toilets were stuffed. I contacted the fire station and had a fire truck come over: I literally used a fire hose to flush the toilets: ugh. As I was doing this, Bp. Caillouet, my former pastor, came to visit me. One of the priests with him came to tell me that he wanted to see me. When I replied, "Let him come see me; I can't leave now, even if I smell terrible," the priest said, "What are you saying?" I answered, "Okay, either you or the bishop can take over this lovely job!" The bishop came to see me. I met him—didn't shake his hand, and asked if I could come visit him to go to confession when I was able to leave the shelter.

Bp. Caillouet (who had ordained me 11 years before and whose assistant I had been before I went to Our Lady of Lourdes) was a good friend of mine. Later I went to visit him at Holy Rosary—he listened to me with much compassion as I described what it meant to have gone thru this experience. And then I went to confession—much relieved and quieted.

Today, as I look back on this experience, as bad as it was, it was nothing compared with Hurricane Katrina 40 years later when St. Bernard parish would be completely underwater for some time, with much more destruction. God, protect us from storms and natural disasters.

## STORY 17: Generous Fun-Filled Souls: Richard/Marceline

My first cousin is Richard who married Marceline while I was a seminarian at ND. Of deep faith and with a beautiful wife, he had very little order in his life: he was said to borrow tools and not return them, so we were told not to lend him any tools, even though he was loved by the family who loved doing things with him.

They had 5 children and worried about having more: the birth control dilemma hit them hard. Marceline once told me, "I am so fertile that if Richard kisses me goodnight, there is danger that, in 9 months, I'll have another baby!" All said with a great smile. Their generosity was so manifest to me that whatever they earned in their rolling-store over a certain amount would be given to me for my seminary expenses. And it was needed.

They were married at least 20 years when one summer afternoon, I was on vacation and installing carpet tiles in my room when we got a call from the Sheriff's office telling us that something had happened to them on Old River. No explanation, only that something serious had occurred, and to go to help. Kearn brought me the message and told me that he would get his aluminum flat boat and motor, and we would go to see what was the matter. Old River is a great fishing lake and one of the oxbows left by the Mississippi where our family loved to fish, ski, and hunt.

Kearn and I drove about 20 miles in his pickup pulling a trailer behind us to a river landing/launch where we launched the boat. We then had to run about 10 miles over that beautiful water to Alligator Point where Richard had a school bus/camp on the shore, kinda primitive, but they loved to go there and spend time together on vacation in that isolated spot, so far away from civilization. To get there by land, one needs a 4-wheel drive vehicle for a 3-hour drive: they had gone there in their fishing boat and motor.

As Kearn and I neared Alligator Point, from a mile away, we could see the bus/camp and near it a tent. Richard was running up and down the river bank, frantically. As we approached, we could see that lying in the door of the tent was Marceline, unmoving, and Richard weeping, praying, and crying. "I killed her! She died while I was getting her another beer—I killed her: it's my fault!" Pain, pain.

Going to her with the Holy Oils, I gave her absolution: she was already turning cold, and then I anointed her and him. We prayed a while, and soon a truck came to us from the woods with a sheriff's deputy and members of their family. It seems that they had gone fishing that morning early and, around the afternoon, returned to their tent to rest and eat. They had a beer together and apparently made love.

He told me, "When I finished my beer, I asked Marceline if she wanted another. While I went to get it and then came back, I found her; her head was turned; she couldn't answer me. It's my fault—I killed her! 0, how I love her—we had so many good times together, and now she's dead! God have mercy on us!" And she wasn't 45 years old—bright, beautiful, deep faith, generous with her family: what a loss.

Richard never got over that. He returned to his store, and when the racial integration happened in New Roads, his store in that neighborhood failed, and he turned to TV repair. His small repair shop was a sort of shack—the light had gone out in his life. He continued taking good care of his children and practicing his faith, but he had been dealt a major blow from which he never recovered. His constant question was Why? "Why her—it should have been me." And still, "You know, Jay, I killed her!" We talked for many hours, many times, but there was no consolation for him.

He later on decided to marry again. His new wife (a grass-widow) was named Margie. The Margie/Marceline names got sometimes confused by him, and that didn't help the domestic tranquility. He died several years later, alone, still grieving by himself. And yet, the surprising thing is that, of his children, all of them graduated from college except one who was a success in his field. That's quite an achievement in our family and town and a tribute to him and Marceline.

## STORY 18: LET'S GO, THE FISH ARE BITING

Daddy loved to fish, and he was a good fisherman. Often, he wanted me to join him, but, when I went home, it was only for a couple of days. I wanted to just "chill out" as we say today.

Being a priest in Violet, with its four missions took a lot out of me, especially in Lent, Holy Week, and Easter. One year, after having had the Holy Week services (with Fr. Schneider doing everything—not asking me to be celebrant, a glorified altar boy), I was tired and wanted to rest. I had heard so many confessions every day, and then, after rehearsing with the altar boys, we had the liturgies, which are tiring at their best (after first hearing many confessions—Easter duties you know), then 9:30 at Yscloskey 8 miles away.

Easter is especially trying—I would leave Violet for Reggio 15 miles away for 8:00 am Mass with the same grind, and then Delacroix Island chapel (another 10 miles), at 11:00 am. Beat back home to eat lunch, then Baptisms at 1:30 pm, all the while wearing the cassock without air—conditioning. When I finished, I drove home to New Roads and arrived late in the afternoon, pooped out.

One of the first things Daddy told me was, "Boy, the fish are almost jumping out of the water to bite on your line in Old River. Let's go get 'em tomorrow. Now that means I'll call you at 3:00 am, and we can be there at dawn." My response? "Please, Daddy. Thanks but no thanks. I'm tired and I want to sleep in." "Listen, man, you won't have this opportunity very often, and you and I can't fish together much, so let's go together. I looked at Ma for help, and she motioned me to say okay. What could I do?

So, at 3:00 am, Daddy called me, "C'mon, boy, get up—you won't regret catching all those bass." "Yeah, yeah, okay." I prayed with all my heart that it would immediately rain buckets, but no-o—it was a gorgeous day—cool, sunny spring day (Easter Monday). I staggered to the bathroom to dress and get coffee. Got into the truck, and we rode to Old River landing where we launched the boat and started the motor. The river was like a sheet of glass.

Halfway across the river, Daddy cut the motor, and we began to string our lines. When he finished getting his rod ready, he put it down, had another sip of coffee, rolled another Prince Albert cigarette, lit it, belched (that was his "fish call" he said), and began casting. His first cast was smashed by a nice bass (about 3 pounds). And I? I tangled my line—then caught a willow tree—then caught the cable holding a log-raft together and had to leave the boat to free my line—also caught the toilet on the raft and then kept casting: no fish.

We fished about two hours. Daddy caught 7 nice bass (which he gave away before we got back home), and I had one strike (which I missed). It was a beautiful day, and the river was so nice. But I capped the climax with one of my last casts—caught another willow tree. What to do? Daddy said, "Point your rod toward the limb and grab the line and pull! Pull harder, the hook must be embedded." "When I did, I yanked it hard, and the bait came flying back at me, and hooked Daddy in the arm! Man, was I sorry—I apologized, and he brushed it off.

Instead, I stood looking at that bait embedded in his forearm. He told me, "Look, get the pliers in my tackle box; we'll have to push it forward until the barb leaves the flesh and then we can cut it off and pull the bait out." Sounded simple—I had done it before on myself, but this was going to hurt my Daddy!

We worked at it without much success and finally got it done: a little bloody, but not much. By that time, I was feeling kinda light-headed. Daddy told me, "Boy, you sure can't take it. I thought you could handle that, but I guess you can't." I wanted to drown myself by this time. If it had been on me, I would have done it easily, but THIS WAS MY DADDY!

I never had the opportunity to clear that up with Daddy. He had a high tolerance of pain (which we all inherited from him and Mom), but I don't think he understood what was Happening.

I did not enjoy that fishing trip but said nothing. I would love to be doing this today with Daddy, but God has had other plans. May he rest in peace.

# STORY 19: 50 YEARS—AIN'T GAWD GOOD?

In the Biblical Book, Ecclesiastes, Qooheleth speaks these words, "Vanity of vanities, vanity of vanities; all is vanity . . . The sun rises, and the sun goes down; then it presses on to the place where it rises . . . but the world forever stays," and "One season following another, laden with happiness and tears." And so it sometimes seems to us. But is that vanity? How time so frequently seems to be such a mystery, especially in its passage, as we age and reflect upon it.

In this story, I would like to surface some of my impressions coming out of my Jubilee of 50 years as a priest and its celebration at Holy Spirit. Our people, led by Deacon Tom Guntherberg marked the occasion "laden with happiness and tears," giving me and us much joy and gratitude. Somehow it seems that this is a prosaic thing—if you live, time goes by, but not many people are able to live this long. (In our priestly ordination class of 12, in 2004, 4 had already gone to God). So this not-so-frequent happening was special after all. My brother Jerry and Adley already celebrated their 50th Anniversary 4 years ago, and now much of our family was here to celebrate with us.

There was much planning going on, unbeknownst to me. Rather, Deacon Tom told me one day, "Why don't you take some sort of vacation—you seldom do—and go somewhere for this week?" So, obediently, I went home to New Roads and the family. Little did I know what was being planned. I knew that many friends past and present were being invited for that date, but that was the extent of it that I knew of.

That Sunday, June 3rd, 2004, I returned from home to find many sorts of strictures—"Don't look this way; don't walk there; we need to put blinders on you; turn your eyes away!" I walked into the kitchen and found a beautiful new fridge (with thru-the-door ice and water), and that was only the beginning. I knew that there were many people around, but I was obedient. I didn't look.

Then came the time for the 11:00 Mass when I was blinded, led by the hand, and urged to keep walking around to the front of the church where, people after people came by to shake hands, kiss, and hug, and then I was permitted to enter the church vestibule.

"Now you can look!" New baptismal font bowl, different lights, stained-glass windows, beautiful bronze stations, new vestments, a lovely stained-glass Holy Spirit bay-window and many people, some of whom had years ago moved away and come back for the occasion. What can one say when all that is revealed? The generosity. Deacon Tom, Joan Brennan, Pam Kamphuis, Fran Laudun, Charlene Vernotzy, with their many helpers, had done the unexpected, and it was great and was completed in only a week.

After the Mass (and me missing Daddy and Mom), Tom called me to the pulpit, and he handed me keys. Keys to what? Big surprise: A golden Buick LeSabre, called the "nifty-50," the car I would have wanted if I had bought it myself! While Pam drove me back to my garage, exulting, the crowd moved to the Parish Life Center Hall for a whoopee!—Band music, ice-sculpture, much food, lovely decorations, and many people signing a huge photo of me smiling at the camera. It's hard not to be overcome with gratitude, joy, and satisfaction.

Sometimes 54 years doesn't seem like a long time, once you're there. As I look at my classmates from the seminary, however, we are getting so o-1-d (not me of course). Surgery does have a way of reminding one of the fragility of life and health.

I've been so healthy all my life: good teeth, hearing, vision, bowels, strong legs which continue to hold the promise of several more years at Holy Spirit. The results of the Storms and the closing/twinning of the Archdiocesan parishes do give one pause as to the future. The unsettling mood of this time brings with it the fragility we experience as we minister for many years.

One never knows where we'll be from year to year, but with such joys remembered from the past, we can only look forward with hope. God has been so good and continues to call us—to the sick, the poor, the aged (among which we now are!), the unemployed, all who need our care and concern. Jesus said, "The Son of Man has come not to be served but to serve, to offer his life as a ransom for the many." May we continue trying to do that, in good health.

## STORY 20: Special People—Sr. Paula Richard

Of all the people who have touched my life, I must include Sisters: the Sisters of St. Joseph (all thru my high school days), the Sisters of Notre Dame at Madonna Manor (where I worked with the youngsters for 2 years while a seminarian), and especially the Eucharistic Missionaries of St. Dominic. As a seminarian in 1950, I got to know them while teaching catechism with them in St. Bernard. And, as a companion to me in my life as a priest, Sr. Paula Richard has had the most influence on me, my spirituality, and my ministry as a priest.

In 1957, I was in Our Lady of Lourdes parish for only 3 months, when Mother Margaret and Sr. Louise Villere came to visit Fr. Schneider and make final arrangements for Sisters. He had applied to get them to live in the parish to teach religion and be a presence there. I didn't know them at that time but would soon get to know and love them and all their Sisters. For years, every week, they commuted the long distance from their Motherhouse, off Magazine Street in the city, to go to the many schools in St. Bernard—a long and grueling trip by beat-up city busses with heat, mosquitoes, and very little support.

Sister Paul Richard, as she was known at time, was a young Cajun Sister from Brusly St. Martin (along Bayou Lafourche), French-speaking, dedicated, bright, and good-looking. She was still going to St. Mary's Dominican College to study theology there. With her came Sister Bernard Carillo, a Spanish Sister from the West, who was quiet but also dedicated and also holy—they were classmates. They would live in a house in upper Violet where Fr. Schneider arranged for them to stay until, 2 years later, he would build a convent for them near the church.

With the Sisters and the teachers we recruited, we taught many classes, met with the 5 communities making up the parish, and engaged in ministry among people whom we quickly grew to love. It was a missionary adventure—long distances, mosquitoes, heat, fatigue—but it became a joy working together. They were studying theology and music appreciation and shared what they were learning; in fact, I became so interested in their studies that I began to attend class with them at Dominican College and then at Loyola. This was in the time before 1962 when Vatican Council II was convened in Rome by Pope John.

My association with the Sisters became a strong daily force touching my ministry. Fr. Schneider at the time was a distant, brooding presence who resisted any sort of closeness by me and by the Sisters (and the people of the Parish, too). As time went on, my work with the youth of the many areas of St. Bernard began to reveal to me what "missionary" meant to the Sisters and to me as Assistant Pastor.

Christmas caroling with the CYO, Altar Boys, Boat Blessings, and almost daily catechism classes occupied our time. In the fall of 1957, Fr. John Bahan (Assistant at Our Lady of Prompt Succor in Chalmette) informed me that there was an opening for a Chaplain in the 159th Evacuation Hospital National Guard Unit. He asked if I would like to try that—it was needed, and paid something to implement my meager salary. And that began another story.

Many years later, the Sisters began to delve into the possibility of Associates in the EMDs, and Fr. Roch Naquin and I were asked to be in the first group, and we accepted it. That, too, is another story. Both of us are still Associates.

My interest in continuing my education grew—I needed 6 hours of Math for any sort of degree, so, in 1960, I returned to Loyola to get those hours and succeeded. But my interest in what was happening in the Church and its thought increased in me, fed by the Sisters who offered articles to read and then an invitation to attend classes with them. I accepted. It was so enriching that when Pope John called the Council in 1959, my interest was piqued, and this interest would eventually consume me, leading me to a degree in Religious Education, and Director of Continuing Education for Priests in the Archdiocese.

All the while my association with the Sisters and Sr. Paul (who became Sr. Paula around that time) increased to enrich my ministry (not only in St. Bernard but also at Holy Rosary and other parishes) and my life until today. They went thru the throes of going from religious habits to lay clothing, driving themselves (which earlier was unheard of), and independence-for-the-ministry. They are not school teachers, but true missionaries—social work, nursing, parish administration—meeting the people where they live and work. I admire them greatly.

Today that friendship continues, enriching both our lives—Sr. Paula as a Religious, and I as a diocesan priest, working in two areas, but still affecting both our lives and ministry. After running a Parish at Krotz Springs in the Diocese of Lafayette, she has been Pastoral Administrator in Assunziata Parish in Houma for many years, and Sr. Janie Quatman a Nurse-Practitioner in Houma. They live together there. So many friends have brought us together, and we reach out to them in our own efforts to minister to them, as our lives and our loves deepen.

## STORY 21: HOLY SPIRIT BEGINNING

As the year went along in 1970, our School Board at St. Joseph Benedictine High School in Chauvin realized that, no matter how much we twisted and turned, we would not be able to reopen the school in 1971. We had begun, in 1968, the Lagniappe on the Bayou Fair. People couldn't afford the tuition, so we would not be able to pay our teachers.

This was a heart-breaker—Fr. Charley Pagiughi, the founder of the school 11 years before, had been able to count on funding from the Archdiocese, which we could no longer do. We had about 400 students in the Junior and Senior High. And we faced the fact that, if we did close the school, there would be pain, deep pain. At 46 years old, I was the Administrator and Pastor of a parish of 2200 country Cajun families.

So, we notified the Archdiocese and the teachers and then called the parents to meet at St. Joseph church one night—one of the most painful evenings I have ever spent. I felt like a failure—everyone was applauding Fr. Pagliughi for his "bravery, foresight, and ability" in opening the school and keeping it open for his six years. A classmate of his, who had been an Assistant Pastor with him at St. Joseph's, even presented him with a trophy for "promoting the education of people who needed and had little help." A very low point in my life—I was the slouch in the back.

A delegation of local politicians and parishioners proposed going to Archbishop Hannan to pledge to keep the school solvent if they put up the money needed. (I don't know why, when we first needed and asked for help, they were nowhere to be found)! And the Archbishop reversed the decision of the

School Board and mine and agreed to that proposal. (He told me, "They left happy," and my heart was broken!) So, I gave it all up for the school year of 1971 but knew that it would not reopen for the 1972 session.

Oh, I continued teaching religion every day at school, but had little association with the teachers who let me know that they had little use for me ("He wants to keep the school closed next year"). The coaches, who ruled the school, had high budgets for which they would soon have no funds. It has never re-opened, even today.

Having been in that Cajun parish (a large new church, Missions at Cocodrie—10 miles down, and Upper Little Caillou—5 miles away) for 6 years, I felt that I had nothing left to give them. So, when the Priest Personnel Board asked for a determination, I said that I would be open to another assignment, perhaps as Co-Pastor somewhere. They offered very little (this was January, 1972), so when they suggested that the Pastor of St. Andrew's in Algiers had asked for the formation of a new parish to be cut off from his parish, I agreed to try that and give it my all. No name, no land, no dollar in the bank, and only 149 families, but which would include Tall Timbers Subdivision; Park Timbers was still only woods. I was healthy and ready!

That raised a hullabaloo because the St. Andrew's pastor changed his mind when he couldn't continue having Tall Timbers in his domain. And to top it off, when the appointments came out, I couldn't come there to begin working in the area because my replacement in Chauvin could not come in until August instead of the usual June transfers. So, I was left dangling while there were petitions and crowd-gatherings about "taking away our parishioners, with this unknown priest taking them away from us; and they probably don't do things like we do!"

Another stressful few months. But in August, 1972, I came in to begin ministry at Our Lady of Holy Cross, courtesy of the Marianite Sisters and their beautiful chapel. I had no place to pray and no place to stay. Much overwork, irregular meals, little hope, until things began to pick up. I even taught High School of religion and Bible Classes at St. Andrew's and in the Holy Cross Chapel, even with some of our present-day parishioners, and began to build a framework of great people who responded to my and our need. They saved my sanity.

When the Archbishop realized that we were going to make it in spite of it all, he responded to my question—"What are we going to call this new parish?" He suggested that the Parish meet and send him three names from which he would pick out the new name. Those suggested names were "Good Shepherd, St. Ben's, and Holy Spirit." I felt that there was no contest, and how right this was! A new pastoral council was inaugurated three months later.

All the while, I was living for that first year on Wall Boulevard in Algiers, courtesy of the Marist Novitiate (12 candidates) and Fr. Jerry Murphy their novice-master. I had a bed, a bathroom, a dresser, and little else—the first collection came to $179.12. The friends who kept me going even applauded, especially that 2$^{nd}$ weekend afternoon when I was counting the collection. Landing on my dresser, a football came crashing thru the window, showering me with glass, surprise, and a football (from the kids playing in the back yard)!

Since that time, we have never looked back. We passed the collection only one weekend—since then, people walk pass the basket on their way to pray and contribute to it that way. We don't make a big deal about the narrow boundaries we have, We just offer a place for people to come, be welcomed, be nourished by the Word, and become a strong, mighty Eucharistic community. For the rest of our story, we will await another story: this one was painful enough. But so satisfying.

# STORY 22: MOVING FROM THE MARY JOSEPH RESIDENCE

In 1975, after spending three years at the Chapel of Our Lady of Holy Cross, we realized that we had outgrown the office and classroom spaces we had. It was a good time, a time of growth, and of deepening close relationships. We had "hatched 'em, matched 'em, and scratched 'em"—the work of the priest and flock, and had to move.

The Archbishop secured for us a place next door, at the Mary Joseph Residence for the Elderly, with their beautiful chapel and open welcome, for a year and a half. It was a good time—the 1800 Vietnamese people who came in 1975 became a part of our regular life. When they arrived, they were a pitiful sight, poor things. They were typical aliens, exiles: health problems, no common language, but we had some great hearts to reach out to help them. The Marianite Sisters, Holy Spirit people, St. Philip's Episcopal people, St. Stephen's Lutheran people, and the Woodland Presbyterians—all these pitched in to help them with tireless effort and with great generosity.

They needed everything: a ride to the Public Health hospital, dentists, delousing, a "yob" (job), clothes, schools, and they were ours! One day, several months after they arrived, I realized (even if I was very ill with Pemphigus) that the Vietnamese people, although very devout, were not receiving Holy Communion. When I inquired of the village leader why, he explained that they had not been to sacramental Confession for months. So, I asked him to tell them to wait after the Mass and I would give them General Absolution, and he could supply translation for the language problem.

He explained that to them, and I could see that it sat well with them. So, I told them that they should go to confession when they had a Vietnamese priest, but I was allowed to forgive them in God's name: Absolution. He translated that for me, and then, as they were leaving, they sang the most beautiful hymn as they went home. After that, they were all at Holy Communion. And they were on their way to become such a great addition to our people—they now have St. Joseph Mission at Woodlawn Estates, with a priest and their own cultural and traditional lives together.

Later that year, in 1975, Mother Charles of the Sisters of the Poor told me that they had problems with the Mary Joseph Residence building. The "Algiers phenomenon" of subsidence began to tear at their floors within three months after they moved into their new building. We had to move. Where to go? We got our people together one evening in one of their day-rooms—pool table in the back with our people sitting on folding chairs, on the floor, or just standing. When I apprised our people of the problem, someone asked me, bluntly, "Father Roy, what are we gonna do? Where are we going next?" Sadly, I told them that I had no answer. But God was "rolling his dice."

Several days after that worrying day, I received two letters—one from the vestry of St. Philip's Episcopal church and one from St. Stephen's Lutheran church, down the street. Both said the same thing: "Our buildings are not our own—they're ours only in trust. You have nowhere to go: we have space. Come, worship in our churches; schedules, calendars, rent, can all be worked out in time."

I have never been so impressed with these people who had worked with us settling the Vietnamese and now were offering us a home! That was "Christianity on the hoof."

So, in 1975, we moved again—we had looked over St. Stephen's and St. Philip's Episcopal and saw that the latter would suit us best. So we began offering Mass in their church with great welcoming from these people, our friends. It all began on Sundays at 6: am (Vietnamese Mass); 8:am for us; 9:30 Episcopal; 11: for us. Jesus was so tired after that workout!

And so it went on for three years, without any cross words or problems, and all the while we were growing. I offered Mass in the house where I was living daily, even if bad sick, while taking massive doses of Prednisone—in 1978 I came out of it. Dr. Nesbitt and Dr. Marshall, great friends, said that I was in remission. God is good. Regularly, since I was now Director of the Priests' Continuing Education Committee, we had classes, discussions and workshops. Many of these, like our catechetical classes, took place in our parish homes with stronger growth in numbers and depth.

In 1978, the Archdiocese was able to buy us some land. The Jesuit Provincial House was located on Stratford Place, and the order offered to sell us 2 ½ acres (near to where I was living down the street), and we took it. Home at last. We planned what our church would look like in the vestry room of St. Philip's and decided many things. We interviewed the Architects and the Contractors, and the building began, to be finished and dedicated in 1981, Church and Rectory behind it. 0 happy day! "Quosque tandem, 0 bomine!" No more "How long, 0 Lord?"

## STORY 23: HOW NOT TO MAKE UP TO SOMEONE

Years ago at Our Lady of Lourdes in Violet, there were many lessons to learn—how not to . . . and how to . . . Sr. Paul and Sr. Bernard, CMD, and I had to contend with our old German pastor, Fr. Schneider. He was a true missionary in his own right—a dedicated, tight, crusty, and imperious boss. Quite regularly, he trimmed us back to keep us "in line." We were not to visit "his enemies," or socialize with them, or take their side in their disagreements, and he constantly had something to complain about in regard to them.

One of the things we observed is that in his homilies, he would preach about the people who were not at Mass TO THE

PEOPLE WHO WERE AT MASS! Looking back on it, it borders on the humorous which, I suppose, is the other side of "preaching to the choir." It all came to a head as we approached All Saints Day Mass in the St. Bernard Cemetery on Nov. 1$^{st}$.

Mr. Collins was one of his "antagonists," a Cajun, a Mason, and owner of a shrimp factory in Caernarvon. (We were not to visit him and fraternize with him—which we didn't know at the time). But we surely found out about that—in the church yard in Violet. There was a tree near the garage which had fallen and was leaning on the garage. I heard some yelling outside, and, not knowing what it was about, came out "to empty a wastebasket." I observed the furious pastor with a sweaty red face, holding an axe in his hands and gesticulating. Sr. Bernard beat it into the church, and Paula was standing there—white faced and shook up.

As a "white knight" I came to her defense (I had known her only three months at the time). The pastor was yelling at her in great anger, with an axe in his hand. When I asked him what was the matter, he included me in the tirade. "You people have come in to take my people away from me—you're not obedient; you know that I don't want you to make friends with the people I don't like." And this went on and on, me standing there with the wastebasket in my hands, and this little nun standing there, trembling, frightened to death. (Looking back on it, I don't know what I was thinking—that flimsy basket was no protection for me or her, but it was something to hold and, if necessary, swing!)

Finally, Paula told him, "Fr. Schneider, I don't know what you're talking about, but, if you don't want us to have anything to do with Mr. Collins, we will not." And with that, still trembling, but with her dignity intact, she left to enter the church (where I'm sure, Sr. Bernard was waiting to find out what happened and what to do next). I was enraged—I had been there for only six months (the six assistants who had been assigned there before me had stayed only two years at the most. So, there was a possibility that I would be going out, too).

That evening, I went to see my friend Fr. John Bahan to tell him about this and to ask what he thought I should do about it. He advised me, "Look, remember that he is the #3 ogre among pastors who has been going thru assistant pastors like high weeds. So, have it out with him—but keep your temper: it'll spook him, and you'll get something done with the situation." It was good advice.

# STORY 24: MEG AND THE BOGUE

I can't see how Holy Spirit could have survived and thrived without 2 people who didn't begin with us yet have had such a major part to play in our growth and stability. Meg and Philip Boogaerts came into our lives right after we moved into our present location, in 1980. They live only a block away and adopted me and the Parish. (Of course the fact that we had space for old farmer Bogy to make his large garden here helped a lot.) But no matter.

Meg was one of the first secretaries we had once we moved into our church and rectory. She has always said that she didn't know what she was doing, but I strongly doubt that. Not only was she in the office with her holy sweetness, but our books were put into a business mode, which has grown from her time. The computers would come later, with Lenel Romero, Meg Cahill, and Joan Brennan. Not only that, but Meg did the shopping for the rectory (even if she didn't do her own shopping—Bogy did).

Meg provided good advice to me so often. She was trusted and loved by parishioners and gave us such a good beginning in our permanent location. For the past 20 or so years, Meg has led a large group of people to help minister to the elderly, sick, and fearful poor folks at the Woodland Village Rest Home.

She followed Terry Bailey who began it all but then moved back to Calgary, Canada.

I have seen their patient care as they pray the Rosary, hold Bingos, and help me with monthly Masses in the day room of the home; they even collect gifts of lotions, powder, toiletries, socks, and fruit to make up Christmas gifts for people who have no one to care for or bother with them. This is not an easy ministry—yet, every Tuesday and Friday, about a dozen people go there to sing, pray, even to dance with them, and they say that these people give them such joy.

Now, Bogy is something else. He can do anything, and he does so. An electrical engineer retired from Bell South, he is a kind of farmer. Up even before the chickens, he has had a beautiful garden planted every year—even to getting a tractor to come and till the ground for him. (And of the mounds of produce from his garden, he gives most of it away—to the Jesuits next door, or to me, or, he puts a package in front of the church for people to take home).

Carrying out the plans for the construction with his dog Max, Bogy was there every day with more than enough advice (and beer) to contractors, laborers, visiting priests, and anyone else who might pause as they passed him. He was and is a 6 foot, 7 inch ex-marine who has some very strong ideas about politics, race relations, and anything else that might come up. In back of the rectory, there is a light pole with the grave markings for 5 of their family dogs buried there.

In 1958, there was a fire in the apartments across the canal to the south of us and, in his frenzy to go help put it out, he scaled a 7 ft fence, got caught in it, and ruined his left knee. It would come back to trouble him in later years.

Today, at 83, Bogy still is faithful to the church—his family gave him a "Bogy-mobile," a 4—wheel conveyance which he drives when he wants to go anywhere (he hasn't driven his "pick-em-up truck" in a while, and then, only when he is out to get more logs for his beloved fireplace).

We who live in the northern breeze from his house and fireplace can tell if the temperature is below 70 degrees because the fire will be lit when it comes down that far. Anyone who drives by the Boogaerts home can see the stacks and stacks of firewood above the 7 ft fence. And the tree-people know that he will take only good wood—no trash stuff—and will split it far into the night: he loves sweet pecan wood.

After Hurricane Katrina, I was away for about 3 weeks (Meg, Bogy, and Fran, their daughter nearby, stayed!). While I was in New Roads, I prayed for and wondered so much about Meg and Fran. There was no phone service coming out of here. One day, I got a call from Brother Terry Todd from next door (who also didn't leave but stayed to protect the place from looting). He got Meg on the phone for me, and I was overjoyed. When I asked Brother Terry where Bogy was, he told me that Bogy was on the tractor-mower doing our lawn with a loaded .45 automatic pistol in his belt! He was not molested or bothered by anyone: the neighborhood was almost deserted.

There are quite a few stories about his generator powering his fridge (to keep his beer cold!). He is said to have driven as far away as Boutte to find gas for the generator and even is said to have gotten into a ruckus when he pulled up to the Wal-Mart pump with 8 gas cans. But he's big enough to get what he needed, and did so.

And, as a sequel, Fran Laudun, their daughter, is custodian for our buildings and the People Program. She, too, can do anything, and does so, even to being a guardian angel for her Dad to save him from walking on gimpy knees. She, too, has been a life-saver for us, and we appreciate her work and her presence, and her daughter, Carolynn.

# STORY 25: Part A—SPECIAL PEOPLE— Adley Alleman Roy

My family has provided so much for me and my life—my faith, my memories, and my joys. My 3 brothers have married well and provided us with the sisters Mom did not have. Among these is Adley Alleman from Morganza—a Cajun background. Mr. Evans was a farmer living in a poor home near his fields: the only heat they had for a while was the fireplace. But they were a happy and close-knit family—3 girls and E.J the oldest.

How Adley took such great care of Mom, especially after she passed 92 years old. In spite of many deterrents, she took better care, I think, of Mom than of her own mother.

Adley and my brother Jerry were married in January '54 after Jerry finished Basic Training in the Army and was sent to Orleans, France. How much they must have suffered with this separation, and that same year, Adley became pregnant with Butchie (Lester).

One night while I was home, Mom, Daddy, Pat, and I were praying the Rosary in the kitchen. The phone rang, and, when Mom answered it, from across the room I heard Jerry yelling, "Yahoo!—Mom, I just felt my little child leap in the womb!" That mysterious miracle touched all of us.

As time went on, Brian, Bug, and Stephanie were born, and we all had a part in doing things with them; Jerry and Adley were such great parents. Even today, Adley feeds about 7 people with breakfast—her children from the shop and anyone else who is hungry and comes by. All the while, she completes the newspaper crossword puzzles (and she's so very good at that!),

A major factor in their family life today is their little dog, Leila. Cute, smart, quick, she is the family favorite. Everyone has to be aware and willing to pitch in on her bathroom habits

("Did she go? No. 1 or No. 2? Okay, take the leash and take her out.") One could easily get attached to her presence, and she is such a joy to Jerry and Adley.

Adley has an ability to read people so well. And people respond to her compassion and listening habits. They come by to get pumped, comforted, and "mothered" and leave consoled. She has been part of St. Mary's Adoration Chapel with Bug and Helen and Kearn since the beginning, over 20 years ago. Also, very important, she is a great cook and does it regularly. How we have had such great meals at their home—neighbors come by for food and advice and consolation.

She loves to fish and doesn't get to do it very often, but, when she does, it's like being in heaven for her. She and Jerry have had a succession of camps, beginning at Old River. Junior Perez from Violet gave me a 38' trailer, and Kearn got a truck to go get it and bring it to Old River. His adventure in getting there is a story in itself, but we enjoyed that camp for several years. Next, they built a new camp after a few floods from high water. They then sold it, and got a new trailer which was set up on the Island across False River from New Roads. That, too, was enjoyed.

Then, instead of a camp on the river, they built a party-barge (raft with motor). We had so much enjoyment taking it out on the river and fishing from it. This, too, got old. Now, in the shed in their yard, Jerry has a beautiful boat, which isn't taken out very often. But it's there.

And the camp Jerry acquired is a beautiful house away from the highway near the woods where the family has had such lovely times.

I recall once spending the evening with their children and them. Brian was a tiny tyke—all muscle and brains. Getting ready for bed, his Mom told him that he had to kneel and say his night prayers. She led him. She said, "Now I lay me down to sleep"—"Now I lay me down to sleep." "I pray the Lord my soul to keep"—"I pray the Lord my soul to keep." "If I should die before I wake"—"If I should die before I wake"—"I pray the Lord my soul to take"—"I think I'm going to bed." And hopped into bed to a howl of laughter from us.

Now those children—Butchie, Bug, Brian and Stephie—are working in the shop, and it's going very well. It isn't often that a family is able to maintain this closeness, but they've succeeded, I think, thanks to Adley and her guidance. Jerry still works in the shop, and even Kearn, now that he is retired from the Nuclear Plant and sold his land and pecan trees. He works at the shop doing machine work when they need him. It's a good arrangement for all. Daddy and Mom would have been so pleased and proud. It's called "A.J. Roy Sons Machine Shop."

## STORY 25: Part B—SPECIAL PEOPLE— Jeanie Ortego Roy

When Kearn finally did marry, he chose a Nurse from Opelousas, a beauty from a Baton Rouge Adult Singles Group. We got to know her parents as their courtship progressed. In 1961 they decided to marry at St. Landry Church. I would officiate, with 4 seminarians who would sing during the Mass. I drove with them from Holy Rosary in New Orleans, and all the way, we talked, sang, and joked (no radio).

Meanwhile, the Berlin Wall Crisis exploded, unbeknownst to us. I returned to Holy Rosary to be greeted with the news that my National Guard Hospital Unit had been mobilized, as was Kearn's. He to Fort Polk and me to Fort Sill, in Oklahoma. What a start to a marriage. But he was game, as I was.

Early in their marriage, Jeanie gave birth to Allen (he was named for Daddy), a normal delivery. But then their second child, Scott, was a premature baby, weighing very much below the usual, and the doctors saved him. Today, Scottie is a father himself, living in Abita Springs after Hurricane Katrina destroyed their home in Chalmette.

Their third child, Gerry, too, was a troubled pregnancy, but somehow Jeanie came thru. But then she began to be sick. Without going into all that, it's enough to say that she and Kearn went thru a hell of their own. Finally they found a doctor who did them a world of good, and today, Jeanie is well, a good mother, and grandmother to 5.

One of the joys which I can share in enjoyment with my sisters-in-law for me is when I go home for more than a day. We go to the Casino in Marksville (our home area)—Jerry and Kearn and their wives. We eat well, play, sometimes winning, and then losing it, but we do have fun. It's a way to play together, like the old days.

Last year, Kearn began to realize that taking care of his large land-holding was more work than he wanted to continue doing. And his health dictated a lot of that. His farm is beautiful, very-well taken care of, but demands a lot of work, with little clear return from the many pecan trees which Kearn has studied, planted, pruned, and grafted. He found a buyer who truly appreciates what that land means and loves it. So, Kearn sold a large part of it and now is taking care of his health (even to working in the Shop when they need him and his work). He and Jeanie have a beautiful home at the end of False River, well decorated and kept up.

Jeanie and Kearn are deeply involved with St. Mary's church as Lectors, Commentators, and Communion Ministers and at the Adoration Chapel. They also minister to the homebound and belong to the Kiwanis Club and their social outreach. Adley and Jeanie are in a Pokeeno and other gaming groups where they enjoy being with other ladies who meet weekly to play.

It's a good pastime—Jeanie and Adley are so close—I am pleased. Their family and Jerry's eat together regularly and do things together. One of the places where we saw Jeanie shine, was in 1973—Jerry and Kearn in the shop had decided that they wanted to buy a few head of cattle together. They did so, plus a couple of horses which were kept on the neighboring lot to the shop. They even welded some pipes together to form a big feeding trough for their stock.

And of course the ground around the feeding trough became very deeply muddy so that it was hard to walk there to bring the feed. Yet this soft mud, Jerry says, saved his life.

One day, Jerry, Kearn and 4 other men were standing around looking at their stock (why, I never knew). Jerry decided that he would get his strong tractor and hitch it to the trough to drag it to another clean spot. And he tried, but it didn't budge. So he gunned the motor.

As he did so, the force on the cable attached to the trough pulled the tractor back over upon Jerry. He was pinned under that still running tractor, deep in the muddy ground. Immediately, Kearn ran and pulled the wires on the engine and killed the motor. The other men came up and lifted the tractor off Jerry. (Later on, he said that he had "given up his soul"—he thought he was gone and was unconscious.)

As they lifted up the tractor, they realized that the iron throttle had come down on his right leg and torn the skin. The ambulance arrived soon afterward to take him to the hospital—they could see in the open wound the pulsing artery, unbroken. So many things took place there so that his life was saved. He survived this trauma, but he has been reminded of how serious this was for him and his mobility—even today, he has to wear support hose for his swollen leg.

Jeanie and her nursing skill came into play—she watched over him, nursed him, and took charge. Today, we have about

8 nurses in the family, but Jeanie was the first, and she was a good one. We are so pleased—God be with her.

## STORY 26: A GIFT

Among all the gifts with which I have been endowed, there are different strata. There are spiritual gifts, physical ones, emotional ones, and gifts which may not seem like gifts, but really are of such value to us that, in a sense, they define us. And the one I want to zero in on is that of the ability to read. From early in my lifetime, this has been one which has given me such pleasure and satisfaction, in addition to the information this has been afforded to me over the years of my life.

I really don't remember how it all began—certainly early on in school, we had the usual direction to words and their value. Good teachers, parents who saw the value contained therein, and other people with whom we were associated all proved to us that in words there was much to draw us into a close contact with growth and development as individuals. To be able to read would open us up to vistas of enrichment, of formation, and of information. And, once we caught on to the riches contained there, we, on our own, saw what this current was and where it would take us, and take us it did.

From early on, we were urged to become "educated," a goal which might appear, perhaps, nebulous and tedious. But reading was much more of a facility which was at hand and reachable. It was a skill, a tool, and so much a part of us that we identified ourselves as surrounded by word and unable to exist without this important ability. Gradually, over the years, we assumed, and rightly so, that without this association with word, life would be without joy, meaning, or hope. And that took on a life of its own as we aged and became more experienced.

Reading became more than "something I can do"—it became a part of my being as breathing is. Furthermore, having a Cajun French background, my mother tongue, I could speak and understand only the French patois which was spoken at home. Like other people my age, I could read and write only the English we encountered in school. I could only take a shot at the standard French written and spoken by Canadians and Frenchmen, even if Cajun is a valid language: it's an aural language for me and others like me.

There have been times when my reading has been challenged by other languages. Having had a Liberal Arts education in the Seminary, I have labored over Latin, Greek, French and English, but each of those languages strengthened my grasp of English and gave me a good background for my reading.

Today, there is so much material for us to read and enjoy: computers and the wealth of information afforded us there; audio-books, Ipods, television, and just plain "hard-copy" books at hand. Libraries, book-stores, discussion clubs, and book clubs are there for us to frequent and make use of, all riches for us to grow on. I seldom reflect on what a tragedy it was that, during slavery times, some people were not permitted to learn to read and write: what a tragedy. Now, we can remedy that situation and open this important world for all to frequent.

## STORY 27: Mom's Friend, Mrs. Bizette

One Mother's Day, in 2000, the family agreed that we would get together at Jerry's camp to have a big dinner in honor of our Mothers. Adley told me that if I was early enough, I should pass by the Lakeview Manor Rest Home to pick up Mom and bring her to the camp. If she was not there, it would be because someone had already brought her. So, I agreed.

## "Lemme Tell You a Story"

When I arrived at Lakeview Manor, I went to Mom's room, but she was not there. So, I went up the hall to the Nurses' station to ask about her. Standing in front of the desk was an old lady who was addressing the nurse behind the desk. Her cane, her eye-shade, and her anger told me she was a resident. The nurse looked flustered, as was the lady. She was telling the nurse, loud enough to be heard easily, "You son-of-a-bitch, if you don't do for others any more than you do for me—you don't do sheet!"

What the problem was, I had no idea, but I beat it out of there. I didn't want to know any more than that, and left. When I got to the camp, I found all the family there—playing bourree, barbequing, talking, relaxing, and having a good time. Mom was already there.

I told them what had happened at the home, and we all had a good laugh over it. Mom's reaction? "Oh, that's Madame Bizette. She's a nice lady. I used to bring her Communion every week."

Her time at Lakeview Manor was such a good place for her. They took good care of her; after all, she knew most of the people there and had brought Holy Communion to many of them.

Jerry, Kearn, and I would often come by to get her for a family function—we would enter the day room and then go to her room if she was not in the front. They all knew Mrs. Lucy.

As she neared the end of her life, Mom (who never could tolerate sleeping in the daytime) began to stay in a wheelchair. And we would push her wheelchair to the car where we folded it, she got in, and we left.

But as she got older and feebler (she died at 97 years old), she began to sleep all the time. One day, we came into the day room where there were at least a dozen people there, most in wheelchairs. We asked, "Where's Mrs. Lucy?" (We had gone to her room and found that she was not there.)

Then we realized that Mrs. Lucy was sleeping in her chair, close to us. This was so different from other times. But she was at peace. Her age made her more graceful and always so glad to see us and to visit. Once when I went to visit, I pushed her chair to the end of the hall, and we went outside—it was a pleasant day. We looked past the nice pasture in the direction of home. She looked out, began to cry, and said, "Oh, notre vielle maison; we were so happy there for such a long time. Mon cher, do you realize that I'm only a mile away from my own bed?" It broke me up. She lived a very good and full life, missing Daddy, but accepting it all. What a gift to us were Daddy and Mom—may we be like them.

## STORY 28: LOOKING TOWARD THE SEMINARY: FR. JANSSENS

As I approached graduation from high school in 1946, I began to reflect upon what I was going to do with my life. On Christmas morning, it hit me that I had to decide on what direction my life was going to take as to the future. We had had many priestly vocations in our family (Gremillions, Cheneverts, Lacours, Plauches, Couvillions—all in the Alexandria diocese, except for Fr. Charles Plauche). So, it was not an unusual thing for me to consider it.

When I approached our old Dutch pastor, Fr. Janssens, he stopped me in my tracks when I asked for his permission and help in entering the seminary. His response (I had been an altar server for many years) was, "Why?" (Which I thought was rather obvious!). "Well, Father, I think I would like to be a priest, and I want to enter the seminary to be as certain as I can." Again, a strange response: "Roy, you have three things wrong with you (besides talking too much): "you're an American; you're a Cajun; and you're an Avoyelles parish Cajun!" And until I was ordained eight years later, it didn't get much better than that. I never had a meal at his house—his housekeeper, Mrs. Rogers, was always good to me, but he was cold and distant.

I went on anyway—I was not only accepted in the 4$^{th}$ class, but our class was able to jump a couple of years in school and formation, due to the accelerated system at St. Ben's (from the war years). The war had affected the curriculum to avoid the draft, and this left an open year when the 2$^{nd}$ year of college class was opened). Fr. David and the faculty chose 12 men to jump those years. I was among the group: scared, but willing to try.

As I entered the theology classes, Fr. Janssens began to trust me. He had me take the census of the parish (and that meant up and down False River: about 1,500 families), and I loved the work. Allen Langlois, who entered the seminary with me in the 8$^{th}$ grade, was much more around the church than I was. I had to work in the shop with Daddy and my brothers.

When I had finished grammar school, I toyed with the seminary idea. Jimmy Lacour, from New Roads. was a good friend of mine, and had entered then, while I stayed home for high school. I had asked Mom and Dad about entering at that time, too, but they asked me, "Look, are you sure you want this?" But I was not. So, they asked me to enter high school at St. Joseph Academy, and, if I still wanted the seminary after graduation, then they would agree for me to try it. (Daddy had planned for me to study accounting at LSU for the shop, but I was not cut out to be a bookkeeper, then or now!)

When, as a senior, I asked Mom about my being a priest, her response was great: "Look, if you want to be a priest, you make sure that you be a good one. If not, drop the idea. Daddy would be very proud if you did this. So, give it a try, but do your best." And I resolved to do that, and did well. During high school, I had not really studied very hard, and, on the stage on graduation night, I really decided that I was going to give my classes the best that I could, and did so. I was ordained eight years later, with my First Mass at St. Mary's, in 1954.

## STORY 29: GRANDPA AND GRANDMA—
## the Praying Rabbit

Sometimes the best stories come from someone else's retelling (we really can't resist the temptation to embellish a good story). Anyway, here goes.

Grandpa and Grandma Roy were retired in Mansura, in their 70's. They had had 10 children, my Dad the oldest, living the life of retired farmers on a fixed income. They were comfortable—owning their 200 acres in a nice home along Hwy. 1. They had a large yard divided by a fence separating the backyard from the front yard. The backyard contained myriads of chickens, ducks, geese, turkeys, guinea hens to such an extent that the grass had been picked clean. The front yard was their showcase with rows and beds of flowers (mostly zinnias).

Each morning, after breakfast, they would sit in their front porch rockers praying the Rosary while watching the cars driving by, and pray, all in French. Grandma didn't speak or understand English. Grandpa learned English early in the war years when he came down with Tuberculosis, when he was treated at Schumpert Hospital in Shreveport. They had a pickup truck and a black polished buggy to be taken out only for special occasions and driven only short distances. This is another grandson story which might come later on, if I decide to tell it.

One nice sunny morning, they were seated at their usual place. At prayer: "Je vous salue Marie, plene de grace; le Seigneur est avec vous; vous etes beni entre toute les femmes, et Jesus, le fruit de vous entrailles est benie . . ." A big rabbit slowly came out of the field into the front yard sanctuary to dine on Grandma's zinnias thru the fence along the highway. No break in the praying. "Sainte Marie, mere de Dieu, priez pour nous pauvre pecheurs maintenant . . ." The rabbit stopped at the flower bed and began eating . . . Grandma got up without missing a word, picked up her shotgun and BLAM!—shot him and returned to her rocker, without missing any words in the prayer. Of course she didn't miss: you don't waste any shells.

". . . et a l'heure de notre mort. Ainsi-soit-ils Amen." Then Grandpa left the porch and his rocker, picked up the rabbit, brought him to kitchen where he skinned him, cleaned him and set him in the icebox. They had him for dinner with great relish. A praying rabbit who stayed for dinner.

## STORY 30: THIS OLD (WARM) HOUSE:

I was in the 4$^{th}$ grade at Poydras High School in 1939. We had lived in a house on Red Stick Street where my brother Kearn was born—Jerry was already there. Somehow, Daddy found out about a house for sale on the Morning Side of town, belonging to Mr. Paul Hebert. A very nice house, what today we call a Cajun cottage, on a large lot on St. Jude Street, but with no electrical power, 4 rooms and a path! Today, this looks kinda primitive.

We moved in and soon found that many improvements were needed. The house faced away from the street; it faced a solid board fence where our neighbor who owned cattle brought his mother cows to be separated from their calves-to-be weaned—smelly and most noisy. The front yard was a foot below the rest of the ground and so, when it rained, we had knee-deep water which just sat and turned putrid.

So, Daddy made arrangements with Johnny Joseph to move the house around so that it faced St. Jude Street; it would give us a large back yard with the surface leveled. Jerry, Daddy, and I helped to do the work of moving it. It took much time and hard work. There was a chimney in the wall between the two front rooms (which would be our parents' bedroom, with our bedroom in the other front room). Back of their bedroom was a large dining room whose back wall Daddy removed to make a kitchen/dining room. The front porch was large—the width of the two front rooms—with 4 posts and the front steps, and a beloved swing.

First, we got electric power into the house—not much other than hanging cords, but better than before. Secondly, we got an indoor bathroom, with hot water and a flushing toilet. And then a large back porch with washing machine: the clothes-lines were in the back yard. Even a garage for our car, when we got a car. We were now uptown—still over a mile from the church, and 2 miles from Daddy's blacksmith shop, but we were settled and not renting anymore, and there were 3 sons now.

We were happy in that house—about 4 blocks from False River where we learned to swim; we fished; we hunted there; and we even learned to sail. It became a wonderful haven for us, and we enjoyed it so much. Also, we had space for Alice, our Jersey cow, and her daughter Jane who would provide us with milk, butter, and sweet cream. Twice daily, I milked Alice and walked her to a vacant lot to make sure that she didn't enter someone's yard and eat something she shouldn't. Usually, she had a 40' chain and stob to let her graze in vacant lots. She was quite clever, enough to open the gate to the back yard with her horn and walk to Mrs. Fernandez's who kept sweet potatoes and corn in an open barn, which Alice relished.

Neighbors? The Griffin family from Buras (a tinsmith); Mrs. Thelma Major who became very good friends with Mom and Dad; and Mr. and Mrs. Frank Major, who had me and Jerry to mow their lawns and provide us with spending money. Band practice became an almost daily routine a couple of years later—this would provide us with the gift of music-making: still a valuable gift for us, even today.

This was the house that I like to call "the home where I grew up" from the 4th grade until graduation and then the seminary. The first year that I returned for summer vacation from St. Ben's, Daddy had acquired a 2-acre lot to build a new shop on Morganza highway and, next to it, our new house, built by Uncle Horace Lemoine. Mom has often said, "Ma chere maison—we were so happy there!"

St. Jude street was not paved until much later; it was dusty and graveled. Sometimes, Jerry and I got a ride to school from Mr. Frank Major, a polio survivor, as he drove his black Model A Ford to and from O.B. Laurent's Lumber Yard. Their 2 daughters grew up with us and were part of the crowd in our area. I learned to enjoy reading for pleasure from Mrs. Frank's stash of Life, Reader's Digest, Look, and National Geographic magazines. A phone? We at first had none—Mrs. Griffin had one so that our neighborhood would have one for emergencies (3851): she was so good at doing things like that.

There were many tall pecan trees in our area, which provided us with tasks which would enable us to make some money for our "stuff": we sold the pecans at the stores around us. Deville's Grocery was one which we frequented (near town). I once had a job of delivering groceries from there. Also, I once was a paper delivery boy (on a bike, early in the morning, which was tough for me)—too many complaints about throwing the Times-Picayune into the bushes around their house, or throwing it on the roof, or leaving it out in the rain and ruining the paper. Mostly, we worked in Daddy's shop "Back of Town."

This meant sweeping the dirt floor; clearing away scraps of iron, or washing the lathe, drills and milling machine with diesel fuel to remove dirt and prevent rust. Jerry and I grew to love those machines. In 1947, Daddy moved the shop to where it is today—I was in the Seminary, so he, Jerry, and Kearn carried the load to the new shop, which we had built together. Today, it is a thriving business, employing Jerry (still) and sometimes Kearn, but also Jerry's children: Butchie, Bug, Brian, and Stephanie. Also, they have an extra welder. How Daddy loved that shop and we still do, too.

## STORY 31: DUAL CROSS-COUNTRY FLYING:

It was 1968, and I had been at St. Joseph's in Chauvin for a couple of tough years, pastor and Administrator/Teacher at St. Joseph Benedictine High School. A lot of stress (which is normal when you follow a very capable and popular Fr. Charley Pagluighi) with a large parish and all of its duties. Fr. Willy Todd was my Assistant: together, we were a good team.

I was a healthy 37 year old, serving in a country-Cajun group of people along 35 miles of Bayou Petit Caillou. In January, '67, I encountered Shingles when I returned from Dr. John Plauche's, complaining of "prickly heat." He told me, "Son, prickly heat, in January? Let me see . . . you've got what Cajuns call 'La Centure'—Shingles!" "What do I do about it?" "You suffer!" And suffer I did. None of today's steroid medicines. Took a whole year of using Benadryl to cut down on the itching. Learned many lessons in that time, and still carry the scars on my rump.

Finding that my concentration was getting diminished, I looked around for help from a good Spiritual Director, Fr. Harry Martin. In discussing it all with my brothers, we came to the decision that we would take flying lessons: I in Houma; Jerry and Kearn in Baton Rouge (and their having a dirt strip operating on Pointe Coupee Road not far away from home for them). I still had some GI Bill funds to help finance the lessons. So I attended Ground School and enjoyed the zest of new things-to-learn. A couple of times, I rode with Kearn and Jerry to land and take off from the rather short strip, building our confidence.

## "Lemme Tell You a Story"

My instructor, Phil Donnell, was a good teacher—knowledgeable, experienced and patient.

The first time (which conquered me) I took a $5 ride during which he told me, "You know, I think you'd make a pretty fair pilot!" And I was sold. I began the lessons soon, and, one day, as we came in for a landing, he told me, "Take runway #19, and come to a stop." And he got out—solo! Much fun. I felt like I was an ace.

Things went on from that—regular lessons; walk-around to inspect the plane; shooting take-offs and landings; stalls and handling them—all made for interesting and refreshing changes for me. Kearn and Jerry were doing the same thing in New Roads—they even found a Cessna 170, 4-place used plane, and together we bought it. It's funny how we go down-hill once an enthusiasm takes over—we buy everything connected with it—typical Roy stuff.

One day, Phil and I were on a "dual cross-country" flight. Beautiful weather: a cool, dry and non-threatening day to fly. We took off from Houma, flew over Morgan City and Patterson and headed west for a couple of hours. Then (while I was still on the left side as pilot), Phil began to do some different, unexpected things. He took the maps and covered the windshields all around us. When I asked why, he told me to keep going; he had an exercise for me, and I would soon find out how to solve some problems he would set up. He needed to disorient me.

And disorient me he did: he took over the wheel, turning one way, then another, dropping in altitude, turning in another direction. I could see nothing—he played with our compass, then the instruments so that we were at point zero. Then he let go of the wheel and told me, "Now, I want you to do many things. Take over the plane; straighten out the compass and the gyro-compass; tell me where you are; find it on the chart; figure out your ground-speed; and I want you to tell me within

10 minutes when you pass the runway at Lafayette. Now take over."

When he removed those charts from the windows, I looked around and saw a city to the north of us. So, following his earlier smart tips, I turned the plane and circled the town, saw the water-tower on which I read the name, "Gueydan" and knew where I was. I found it on the map and then plotted my course to Lafayette, to the east. I established my altitude, straightened out the compass, did my math-work on the slide-rule, told him my air-speed and ground-speed, and made it on time over the Lafayette airport. Success. That man really knew how to coax me into doing something I don't think I could have done if he had not prepared me so well. Regularly, he would pull the throttle and tell me, "Now, your engine has quit. What do you do? Can you land anywhere that you can see? Tell me about it."

Later on, our Rectory in Chauvin would burn in 1969, and that ended my flying career: too many things to care about. But it was such fun—my brothers, Mom,, and I would so enjoy flying. (Mom had no fear—open the door, and she hopped into the backseat like she owned it). Today I have more sense—age and wisdom beckon me to let this pilot's license remain in my wallet—I haven't flown in years, and that's all right with me. But it was worth it: there's no experience like it.

## STORY 32: YOUNG PRIEST EXPERIENCES DEATH

For the first three years of my priesthood, I was stationed at Our Lady Star of the Sea (off St. Roch Park, downtown New Orleans), with Fr. Bill Greene. It was a learning time; we had many interests in common, and he taught me much. We had a grammar school, active CYO, Altar Society, Choir, and Altar Boys. These last 4 were my "areas." This was the time of the

3:00 am "Fisherman's Mass" (before evening Masses and air-conditioning).

Regularly, both of us Assistants to Msgr. Joe Boudreaux visited the sick in the parish and brought Holy Communion to the homebound, and there were many. But in all that time, I had never experienced the onset of death or witnessed its effect in the moment of dying. It took place in this way:

Every week when I visited the Rest Home, about 10 blocks from the church, I spoke with, prayed with, anointed, and gave absolution to the residents living there. All of them except Mrs. Ellie. She was aged, a Catholic; she would speak to me, but let me bless her only from across the room. She told me, "Father, I appreciate your caring and coming to see us, but please don't make me go to confession—I'm not ready." And I left it at that in respect for her feelings; we were friends, but no more than that.

So, one Saturday afternoon, about 2, I got a call from the Home. "Please come quickly—Mrs. Ellie just had a bad heart attack and asks for you to please come." I got into the car and raced over there where I entered her room. She was fidgeting around in bed, gasping for breath, and, when I approached her bed, she said, "O thank you for coming, Father. I know I'm dying, and I want to go to confession." I gave her absolution and anointed her forehead, her heart, and her hands.

Before I had finished that, I could see that she had "passed." No more words or movements, and gradually she became relaxed. I closed her eyes, with an appeal for God's blessing on her as she went to God.

It was a deeply moving experience—from vitality, warmth, movement, words, and then to a gradual cessation of anything more than just being there, becoming cold and rigid. I felt privileged to be present and to experience this mysterious reality—a reality which all of us have to walk thru as we go thru the door of death into "somewhere better," the hands of God, knowing him as we are known, face to face.

My love for Mrs. Ellie and my wishes for her to be open to God's boundless mercy helped me to mature into a better priest. We deal with such reality that can become routine and minus much feeling unless we constantly "blow on the coals of the heart to enliven the flame of life itself." I like what I do and what I am.

# STORY 33: A SUPER-NURSE—
## Sr. Janie Quatman, EMD

I don't think that I've ever met someone so "giving" as Janie Quatman. She is a Nurse Practitioner, having gone back to school at LSU and UNO, besides her other schooling. Several years ago, when she graduated from UNO, Barbara and Richard Donlon, Sr. Paula, and I were there to . . . Oh, just to be there and cheer her on. We were so proud of her.

Janie is from Lima, Ohio, the eldest of a large close-knit family for whom she is really the mother, once her mother died. She stays in close contact with her brothers and sisters and also their children whose weals and woes she experiences as few aunts could. Her compassion is boundless; her intelligence and nursing-skills make her invaluable. She works with a few doctors in Houma whose patients are poor, often minorities, and Janie tries to get them help, as she does in a couple of Rest-homes in that area.

Today, Janie and Tony her brother, have bought a house in Houma, and she has made it such a home for herself and for Paula (and anyone else who needs a place, a bed, a shoulder to cry on, or whose spirits need uplifting). She is a holy person whose intelligence and dedication to helping others has made her path sometimes a rocky one. Even I, as well as I know Janie, don't know all of her crosses and crises she has encountered on her way. She has no ego and is content to help out and take no credit for anything worthwhile even when people are raving over her thoughtfulness.

I have known and loved her for many, many years. When I was in Chauvin, ('66-'72), she was stationed in Grand Caillou with Sr. Esther Calderone where our paths crossed a few times. As she went thru her steps to final vows, I did know her, but not well. It is only in rather recent years that I've gotten to know her better, especially thru Sr. Paula who lived with Janie after Janie graduated. She had spent many years before that out west—in Missions in Idaho and Arizona on the native American reservations. She relished that work and those people, as difficult as that ministry was. And then coming to south Louisiana, she took to the Cajun people as few northerners have done, without those funny little "put-down" ridicules that flourish among Sisters and Priests from outside who work in our area. Janie was on the Central Team for a term and it came to naught (I won't go into that). But her relations with the New Orleans people with whom she worked (outside the EMD community) were a joy to her, then and now.

When I came down with pneumonia, Hurricane Rita was headed our way. I thought that I would pass by and pick up the Sisters from Houma and evacuate them to either Baton Rouge or New Roads in evacuation. But Janie would hear none of it—I was too sick, and so I stayed in bed for the duration of that storm, fever and all. We were spared damage or high water—in fact, we never lost power, even though I was so scared that someone would beat on the front door during a night and yell, "It's the Red Cross: get out—the water's coming up!" It never happened, and we were grateful. Regaining my health, I came back home soon after it passed us. Super-nurse brought me back.

# STORY 34: WILLY MERIDIER: FROM SOLDIER TO PRIEST

Wilfred Meridier graduated from LSU in 1961 and went into the Army Reserves. To his surprise (and to that of the whole National Guard 159 Evacuation Hospital unit to which I belonged), the Berlin Wall Blockade demanded that we be federally mobilized that summer. And so we headed to Ft. Sill, Oklahoma, a table-top, windy, hot plain, to run the Hospital there.

Before that, I attended Chaplain School in New Rochelle, NY for several weeks, and returned to the unit the day before we were sent to the boonies for a Unit Test in the hills (42 large tents, with all the mobile equipment that a hospital has to have). The next day, the temperature dropped to 5 below. It was some cold for us New Orleans boys. But we were young, in good health, and so Gung-ho that we took it all in stride.

After we were set up a few days later, we began to go thru the many tests and drills to be certified. It was a lot of spit and polish, but we were snug in our sleeping bags with air-mattresses at night and fresh hot food in the daytime. I said Mass in a tent where I noted that the kneeling men who served the Mass left melted spots in the icy snow on the floor: our canteens tinkled with the iced-up water we carried.

One morning, I got up early before most of the unit and went to the kitchen with my helmet for hot water with which to shave. After that, I finished dressing and decided to go out in the early dawn to see what the country looked like. It was beautiful in that dawn as I walked to a nearby hill in the snow. At the top of the hill was a gun-emplacement with a guard standing there on duty. I called out to him, "Hey, it's Fr. Roy—good morning!"

The answer came back, "What's good about it? I'm cold, and I'm tired of this foolishness." "What are you doing?" I asked.

"Well, here I am, guarding this g—d—empty machine-gun here in this nowhere, with an damned empty gun. Now that is what I call 'military intelligence'—this makes no more sense than us being here in this ridiculous place." How do you answer that? Later on, I would tease him about this exchange (in fact, I told this story decades later at Willy's funeral when he died of ALS (Lou Gehrig's disease). We became good friends. In fact, he and my chaplain's assistant Wayne Oubre and I would have many good meals together as our friendship grew during that year.

One night when we were just hanging around in the field, off duty, Willy asked me about the seminary. When I asked why he wanted to know, he revealed to me that he was thinking about the priesthood and wondered what I thought.

We ended our term at the end of that year, Willy entered the Pope John Seminary, and in 6 years he was ordained to the priesthood. I preached at his first Mass at St. Leo the Great parish in New Orleans. He was a good priest, constantly taking courses in theology and spirituality at Loyola Institute of Ministry and keeping up. God rest his soul; he left many friends in and out of the priesthood. Thank God he died before the evacuations for Hurricane Katrina in 2005.

## STORY 35: STORIES PRIESTS USED TO TELL

"Dese days . . ." is the expression in our post-2000 years. In the "old days," we had so many occasions to get together and exchange stories. First of all, there were more younger priests than we have today. Although we were unaware, we were homophobic, sexist, snobbish, and racist, as I look back at myself. We had much to learn.

Our class had 12 ordinands (six from the Archdiocese); there was even a class of 18 (six celebrated their 60th anniversary this year). Also, in the old days, we had Retreat times, Junior Clergy exams, 40 Hour Devotions, and Confirmations, during which times there was usually a big dinner around tables where stories were exchanged. And we can't forget the characters, some still around who not only told the stories, but about whom those stories were told.

To name a few—Charley Pagliughi, Jerry Mire, Poopsie Daigle, Pete Bergeron, Benny Bendix, and even Winus Roeten, who not only told the stories, but they had stories told about themselves which were also popular.

And of course, there were others about whom many stories were told. Bp. Abel Caillouet was a favorite. He was our Auxiliary Bishop, while his brother Lucien was the Vicar-General (they were called "rigid"—Lucien's arthritis and "frigid"—the Bishop). For myself, I've always had a great regard for the Bishop whose Assistant I was for almost four years, and who ordained us instead of Archbishop Rummel whose blindness made that not possible for him.

Bp. Caillouet was always "proper/formal"—Victorian, unsmiling, a demon when it came to ceremonies, but whom I found to be a very dedicated and zealous pastor at Holy Rosary and, from what I heard, in the Houma area and among the Cajuns (where he was born). He had rules, and, come hell or high water, he was unswerving. He was not mean (as we heard about some of the Ogre meanie pastors who were still around in our time). We always knew where he stood—he was persnickety about dress and liturgical ceremony, but while living with him, once we knew the rules and kept them, he was not unpleasant. The people loved him and his devotion—he worked hard for his people.

I experienced this story myself. We had a 6$^{th}$ grade teacher named Mrs. Oddo. One day, as she entered her classroom, she was shocked to see written on the board "Oddo is fruit." Of course she got angry: she seated the class (of about 30 kids) and berated them. "I know that some of you did this, and I want the culprit to come forward to tell the truth." Silence, and no one moved. "I'll give you 5 minutes, and, if the guilty party doesn't admit it, I'm going to call Sr. Judith, the Principal, in and she'll give you your what-for." Nothing.

So, Sr. Judith came in, furious. "Who did this? You'll stay in until we find out who had such little care about our good teachers that they would say such dirty things about them." Still nothing. "Ok, I'm going to get the Bishop, and he'll get to the bottom of this mess." (I found out about this fracas and stood, hidden, in the hall to watch—it was too good to miss,)

The Bishop swept into the classroom—full Bishop's rig—cassock, belly-band, chain, skull-cap, and ring. Ominous. "Good morning, Bishop!" Brooding "Good morning, children. Be seated. Sister tells me that someone has no respect for our church, our school, our dedicated teachers."

"It is a shame that, in our day of a good education and the great sacrifices that your parents have made for you, that somebody has no respect. Surely, you must understand that this writing on the board shows that all this has been wasted on someone here in this classroom. 'Oddo is fruit.' Wrong! Don't you know that you must say, 'Mrs. Oddo'"?

By that time, in the hallway, I could hardly contain myself—he had missed the whole point. But that was the Bishop. Innocent, naïve. And yet, he blithely walked away. The incident was never settled, but we priests had a good laugh in the telling about it all.

## STORY 36: CHAUVIN FRIENDS

There have been times in my life when I felt that I was under the point of the pyramid turned upside-down upon me. At those frightful pain-filled times, I also have realized that I have not really looked at the great people who made it possible for me to survive those times. And I now realize the rich friendships which were given to me and to us.

Chauvin and my six years assigned there had many such people who made the journey with me and who are still there. They underwent with me the closing of St. Joseph Benedictine High School, and they still bear looking at that now empty building. They helped to begin the Lagniappe on the Bayou Festival to keep the school going; they moved it to grow almost out of sight; they watched as Bp. Boudreaux removed that sort of fund-raising from the church parishes and went along with it. And still they maintain their faithful presence to the church and its people. Among them are:

Odis and Janice LeCompte: Some of the greatest friends I have ever had in the world. I would entrust myself completely to them, without any hesitation. They are holy, beautiful, smart, hard-working, and immensely good. A large family, great Catholic sense, stable, and a whole lot of fun to be with. I am so deeply indebted to them and their families.

Del and Mary Britsch: Another family whose faithfulness to me and to the church saved me from much grief, pain, and challenge. Always seeing so clearly where truth lay, and willing to support even the mistakes I might have made with the school and the people who taught there. Still they live there—all I would have to do is to call, and they would be on the spot. Like the LeComptes, they have suffered bad storms and floods and still live there so fully.

Imelda Pellegrin: Closer to me, I think, than my blood family itself. We have together gone thru so much of life-challenge, threats, but also so much of good living. Myo died this year, and their large family was like my own. With her close friends, Bella Authement, Merle Lirette, and Helen Lirette, Imelda is a saint: gentle, intelligent, humorous and so giving. Without her and these others, I fear what would have happened to me and my ministry.

Sou and Helen Lirette: Again, it frightens me to think of what I asked of those people. They gave me and the church their time, their hard long-lasting labors, their imagination, and their open, good friendship. I will always be grateful for that: it isn't often that one runs across people of such quality.

Gerald and Judy Duplantis: quiet, steady, trust-worthy friends, who made living such a joy, even if facing great difficulties, without any solutions in sight. Yet we all hung on. The friendships have lasted, and I think, gotten more golden with time (it's now been 36 years since I left Chauvin—but my heart still is there, thank God).

Mary Francis (Sr. Mary Basil, OSB): Mary and Bob Francis now live in Mississippi. Mary was a strong support with the Chauvin bunch for me to be able to survive the events which transpired there from 1967-'72 and the school closing.

Some have gone to God: Jacob and Buddie LeCompte—Noncle Jake Exposito—Annassee Authement—Easton Pellegrin—Fr. Charley Pagliughi. All these have a place in my heart, and I pray for them so that I, and we, don't make the same mistakes as in the past.

And not to forget—Tommy Smith. A man (and priest at that time) who stood with me when there were few people (I thought) close to me who could touch and support me as Tom did. We worked well together and were on site when Big Joe Chotin and Jack Monteleone did their number in Chauvin. Much of what we saw we still don't understand, but leave it all in the hands of God. Joe has now gone to God, this year, and Jack is now a priest in the diocese of St. Petersburg, Florida. God bless them both.

Leonard Chabert: I've had a lot of animosity toward this man and politician but have tried to overlook much of it. I think I've forgiven the machinations of those days: it was rather fierce for a while. And now that the school is closed (and Leonard has passed away), it's all behind me and us. This man was instrumental in acquiring the Leonard J. Chabert Hospital in Houma, and that is a great credit to him. His family remains in Chauvin.

## STORY 37: VIOLET FRIENDS: Mrs. Perez and Ruth Maloof

It seems that in every pastoral assignment I've had, there have always been persons whose dear presence have gifted me and the parish, unexpectedly and generously. Two of these people were clearly saints, and each had a part to play in my life.

Mrs. Manuella Perez, wife of Merrill Perez, was one such person. She was the backbone of Our Lady of Lourdes Parish, living in Violet—daily Mass, food and friend for the hungry Assistants and Sisters, and a family who took us in as one of them. This means praying, playing, and supporting, whether in a duck blind, or a catechism class, or just listening to and "carrying" all and each of us. This had gone on for many years, and that included Fr. Schneider. Mrs. Perez went into Altzheimer's and sadly died over 10 years ago. Her expression: "Don't worry about nuttin.'"

Another dear friend is Ms Ruth Maloof, of Braithwaite. Ruth was also one who provided food and loving support for priests and Sisters, especially Sr. Paula Richard. Her mother, Momma Maloof, was a Lebanese member of the Orthodox Church and a great friend. Ruth has been thru a very difficult time with the storms. She was Postmaster for many years and retired about a dozen years ago, with a beautiful warm home, but she is now bed-ridden and has to have a daily sitter to be able to make out. I speak with her on the phone a couple of times a week—she is lonely and has enough of being bed-ridden. She is so dear: a saint, too—an Associate of the Eucharistic Missionary Community although she has been unable to do much except answer the phone when we call. I visit and anoint her; it's quite a distance, but I try.

In 1958, Ruth, Mrs. Perez, Mom and I took a beautiful western trip to Yellowstone Park and the environs. It was a great trip—we have joked about me being cooped up in a car with three women for a couple of weeks and being so relieved when we came back home. Not really true. But it was so enjoyable, all four of us being such close friends.

Mrs. Perez's family is beginning to die off—Rabbit, Junior, Alfred, and Edouard are already gone. The younger members of the family have taken over the Better Boxing Company for the past several years. I've thought about Junior's death this year—when he gets to heaven, he'll have a large priestly company waiting for him—Fr. Schneider, both Finnegans, Hubert Brou, Henry Naquin, Murph Bordelon, Benny Beninato, Carmel Grech and Poopsie Daigle, plus his parents—he was good to all of them, as was Rabbit and Alfred Henderson. I'm sure that the humor and the jokes will continue, as they were when we were together in Violet.

Ruth's family was an unusual one—of the 5 Maloof girls, Ruth was the only one who did not marry—she provided help with the grandchildren of her sisters, and now that she is ill, they provide help with her and her well-being, one of whom is Leonard Bazile. He and Charlotte, his wife, evacuated her to Memphis, then to Shreveport, then to River Ridge. In the meantime, they cleaned out her flooded home and then moved her back into it. They are repaying her for her great care for them when they were younger. These friends have been priceless, and I am grateful for their gifted presence in my life.

## STORY 38: A STRANGE IRONY

When Hurricane Betsy arrived in 1965, we went thru a whirlwind of our own in St. Bernard Parish. We spoke about this in a previous story. I was Shelter Manager and remained there in the high school for two weeks until the Red Cross came in with personnel, water, radios and supplies.

In that fearful time, there was much stress as we dealt with the fears and uncertainties of so many poor people who not only did not know what had become of their homes and possessions, but they had no way to getting back "down the road" except in a boat. A thousand people, jammed together without showers, operational toilets, and direction was a frightening situation. We managed it—so many people of good intentions and willingness were there to support good order.

But during that time, I very soon lost my voice—hoarse, and yet I still had to use that precious voice to communicate without a bull-horn to the many areas where people were bunked down. It was so hot; there was no ice for our medicines and no power, and tempers were short.

My voice was gone for the next 20 years—never the same strong, loud (sometimes) and comfortable voice. I could sing, but not very much—just speaking was in a strange sound.

In 1966, the Archbishop asked me to be Pastor of St. Joseph in Chauvin, with its Junior/Senior High School for which I was Administrator—a very stressful assignment because I had never done any "administrating of a school and a parish." The Faculty was an amalgam of individuals: teachers, coaches, choir director, Assistant pastor, and Benedictine Sisters. I was always wondering if I was doing the right thing for the school and our teachers, without any feedback from some who really could have helped me to bear the load. The School Board which we founded was such a support, though, with the friends of the school, but still, there was stress (mostly financial). And that didn't help my voice.

After being there for six years, we reluctantly accepted the decision that we couldn't re-open for the 1972 school year. More stress, and heavy sense of failure: anger ("He closed our school"). Then, having the rectory burn down in January, 1969 complicated it all. But in October of that year, our school had a Visitation by the Southern Association of Schools and Colleges for accreditation, which we passed. From this, I was able to get a Masters degree in History from Notre Dame Seminary to benefit the academic standing of our faculty.

All during this time and activity—in church, school, and daily living—I was using my voice, which sometimes amounted to a squeak. Then in 1972, Holy Spirit Parish was founded, and we entered another episode of development and journey. Still no voice.

Illness began during the week of Thanksgiving, 1974. Severe sore throat and deep fatigue led to a doctor visit by Dr. Jose Torres who came with penicillin and vanilla ice cream. Three months later, it came back; and three months another bout. Finally, Dr. Torres advised me to see an EENT doctor, Dr. Ullo, in Marrero: it was more than strep throat.

Another adventure—he told me that it was not strep throat that I had, but seemed to be something more sinister Pemphigus, an auto-allergy. What to do? Visit a dermatologist—Dr. Dan Marshall and Dr. Lee Nesbitt—who told me that "this is endemic to Eastern Mediterranean Jews"!! Lee and I have laughed about this many times. A great friend and great doctor.

And that began a regimen of doctor visits, tests (allergies especially), but not much of any decision. "What do I have, doctor?" "I don't know, Father, but we'll cure you!" Sigh.

Then I began with Prednisone—40 milligrams, then 60, then 100 a day. I had developed sores in my mouth, my throat, even my face and eyelids. I'm sure that I didn't smell so good either, but never heard any complaint from the people around me. They were so kind and caring. Dr. Jerry Ryan and his wife Rosie were so good to me—Jerry even told me that unless I underwent voice-rest, I would lose my voice completely. So he called the Archbishop to report this, and I went to St. Ben's for a 6 week period to rest it. A profound retreat for me, my guitar, my Bible and my spirits, with the good friends among the monks at the Abbey.

At St. Philip's Episcopal church where we were ministering (for 3 years), I even whispered the prayers, and Denis Grace would speak then into a portable mike so people could hear. And it worked!

Finally, I took my last dose of Prednisone in July 1976, the night I got my Masters in Religious Ed from Loyola Institute of Ministry. Couldn't take a swallow of champagne the people gave me because "the doctor says I can't have alcohol." "Take it; we're nurses, and we say you can have at least a swallow." So, I did.

And then strangely in time, something began to happen. I began to develop some of the symptoms for which they prescribe Prednisone—hearing loss, arthritis, glaucoma, and asthma. But what really surprised me is that I started to get my precious voice back! I could sing; I could speak (and preach), and teach. Why?

It was then that I realized that, because of the asthma, I could not overpower my voice anymore (because of the lack of breath support). As long as I had a voice, I could put up with the shortness of breath. And that's the story of "the 2 sides of the Cross." I had to be very careful with my breathing, and I had to use the voice sparingly, at least at first.

And it was then that I realized what St. Paul had to say, "When I am weak, it is then that I am strong, for Christ is with me." And asthma made it possible for me to once again sing and speak. What a gift to have returned to me. I am grateful.

# STORY 39: A BAFFLING ENCOUNTER: "Out of the Blue"

Sometimes when we least expect it, help comes to us. [Someone has said, "Grace comes to us, not before we need it, and not more than we need."] This is a story of such help.

One Labor Day, I was scheduled to offer the 4:30 pm Mass for the EMD Sisters at Regina Coeli Convent, outside Covington, where they were having some sort of pre-Chapter gathering. So, after I said my second Mass at Holy Spirit, I drove over the Causeway in the early afternoon. While on the Causeway, I noticed that my dashboard panel light came on. I tried to ignore it and kept driving until I came into the Regina Coeli convent yard.

When I came to a stop and parked, the dash light remained on—telling me that something was very wrong with the electrical system of the car. I tried to re-start the car, and it gave me some difficulty, although it did start. I knew that if I didn't do something about it, things would only get worse. Consulting others better versed in "auto-stuff," I was advised to drive to Covington (about 5 miles away) and get help while the car was still running roughly; so I did, without air-conditioning and with much trepidation.

On a Labor Day holiday weekend, don't look for help—stations and dealers are closed and traffic is dense. The car stopped twice on the way: I was able to re-start it, but I knew that I was in for distress. Arriving at a Wal-Mart store, I found that nothing was open except for a person who told me that he would be able to sell me another battery, but nothing more.

Dead in the water. I was stopped, the car hood open, a very hot sweaty black-suit, Roman collar and dirty hands, and not at all knowing what else to do. Desperate and exposed.

All of a sudden, a pickup truck came around to my car and stopped. The young fellow who came out was shirtless, with flip-flops, and a brash look. I had no idea what was taking place. He came over to my open hood and looked in. Then he told me, "The Lawd has sent me to help you." I was not impressed at all.

He said his name was "Brandon." And continued, "I had the same problem with my own car a few weeks ago. I will help you. You seem to have a dead alternator; I have the tools and I know how to fix it." What do you say to that? I thought to myself, "O great, this is what I really need—some sort of red-neck country preacher who is going to make my afternoon even more stressful than it already is and will run me up some blind alley and leave me high and dry!"

When I murmured OK, he got his tools and removed that gadget and motioned me to get into his truck. "To go where?" "To Auto-Zone—I know the people there and they can check your alternator and sell us another one." So, we took off, and, while driving, he told me about himself. It seems that he worked for a trucking firm in Covington and New Orleans, and on the side was studying to be a preacher. All the while, I was giving myself into the hands of the Almighty because I was completely at Brandon's mercy—unknown, and all the while hoping that this was a good idea. But I had no other choice.

Within minutes, the Auto-Zone people did check my alternator, which was defective, and brought out a new one, which I paid for with my credit card. We returned to my car at Wal-Mart where Brandon re-inserted it and connected it up.

He got into my car, the engine turned over, and it worked! "Halleluia!" Brandon was not surprised or excited but went on finishing it up as if he expected it to do just that.

When I got into the car, much relieved at the unexpected solution to my mess, I offered to pay him, but he would hear none of it. "The Lawd sent me to help you, so I can't take anything for that. Have a blessed day." And he drove off. All I could give him was a delicious cold Coke. And I got back on the road to the Sisters, in time for that 4:30 Mass, completely relieved and ashamed that I had misjudged him, his intentions, and his ability, coming out of nowhere.

I did get to repay him—he had told me that he worked for a firm called "Rollins Trucking Company," so the next day I called them and asked about him; I got his full name and address and sent him a check for what I thought was adequate payment.

I've prayed for him but never have heard anything further about such a Good Samaritan. I prayed that I might be able to help anyone who would also be in such a desperate situation as I had felt I was in when he came to pull me out and get me on my way. God bless him on his journey.

## STORY 40: THE STRENGTH OF MUSIC FOR ME

As I look at my life, I see that there are a few influences which have so major a value for me. One, of course, is my Faith (probably the most important one). The other is Music: playing it, singing it, and enjoying it as it carries me along.

The earliest "musical happening" that I can remember took place when our family lived on Red Stick Street. This was in—I think—1939 or '40 (I was at Poydras High School, near where we lived). On Red Stick were two black brothers—Cocky and

TiMorceau (Cho-Cho). Cocky played the drums. One day, as I passed his house, he was playing his drums by himself: no music. I called to him, and he invited me in to listen. While I was there, he had me sing "The Isle of Capri" while he kept time on the drums (and he was pretty good). From that time on, he called me "Isle of Capri."

We always sang at home and at school. Daddy played the violin and the guitar—he had a great ear and played well. Mom, of course, sang (one of the things we remember is that she said, "When I get up in the morning, with my prayers, I sing one of the hymns we know, and then for the rest of the day, it continues to go round my head").

Morganza always had a band, and they had good musicians. I think it was 1940 or '41, a group of New Roads people got together at the Woodmen of the World Hall to try to form a band. Daddy, Misters Niland, Roger and Humphrey Olinde, Bert Lieux, Alton Gaudin and others had someone in to help us, and they brought in instruments. Jerry got a saxophone; I got a Leedy snare drum. It was a good one (I seem to think it cost all of $30), and I prized it.

When we got home, we were assured by our parents that we would have to practice. "Music instruments were not something to play with, but to be 'played on'," and enjoyed with band-director (Mr. Thornton), and we both were serious about it.

Band Practice twice a week after school—both our schools in New Roads (St. Joseph and Poydras) made up one band—the practices were in the Poydras Auditorium, with about 50 members. New Roads didn't have much in the line of sports outside of school—the war came along, and it drained our young men from town, so band became a highlight.

Regularly, we would give concerts at Poydras school. Then came Prof. Erny—a good director who loved more than anything, a marching band. He drove us—practice sheets which would have to be reported on with demerits for failure to practice. (My poor parents had to put up with my practicing at home—imagine the drum and my keeping time and putting in the time in practice). But being 1$^{st}$ chair Drums meant that I could lead the band, keeping time both when the band played and when I kept cadence as we marched. Oh, how that was glorious—even Jerry thought that was fine. We would practice musical sections together: horns, reeds, brass, etc., and we grew in appreciation and enjoyment of "making music." (Of course, Jerry's life-blood was in the shop—fixing things as Daddy did, and Jerry—later Kearn—caught the bug and kept it.)

Daddy knew Johnny Joseph, a black man who really played the drums well, and got him to give me some lessons. He had me concentrate on "rolling the drum," and I got to be pretty good at it. Another lesson he insisted on was the "after-beat." Today in our popular music, the after-beat is prominent. As I neared the Seminary, Daddy got me into a Country Music Band—"Dumpy" was the leader—we played at River's End for Mr. Joe Chenevert. From this Sunday night music, I paid for my books and clothes into the Seminary—a borrowed bass drum, and cymbal, and I owned my own foot-pedal. It was a spectacle to think of me covering my drums when a fight broke out on the dance-floor, as I protected them.

Mardi Gras in New Roads began to blossom—Jimmy Boudreaux, a black man, would march ahead of the band, and wave his baton as we marched the miles with him. It continues today, with many bands, floats, and crowds: two parades on Mardi Gras.

There are few thrills more profound for me than to be part of something harmonious, whether it is playing music or singing it. And it has continued—the bands I have been in, the Glee Club with Fr. Naughton, the choir of Elise Morel, and the Schola Cantorum in the Seminary, St. Ben's, and Notre Dame.

When I left home to St. Ben's, I sold my drum, and hated to see it go, but it had served me well, giving me a taste of something whose enjoyment nothing else would provide me. And music continues today to give me that "pearl of great price." Either I'm humming something, whistling it, or singing it. It's a part of what I am.

I played the drums in the seminary band; early in the seminary I got a ukulele and learned to play it as I worked with youth in my ministry, starting in 1950, when Don Byrnes and I worked with the youngsters at Madonna Manor. Singing on a bus as we drove somewhere with them was helped along with the uke or the banjo. This continued for many years.

In 1969, when the rectory in Chauvin burned, I gave up my phonograph and records and decided that I would buy a guitar and lessons from Bill Brasher, a teacher in the schools who taught the Terrebonne Parish children with his guitar (an Ovation). He was good and helped me learn, and this became another step in "music formation" for me. Now arthritis has taken over, and all I can do—besides owning the guitar—is enjoying the music and keeping up my musical ear.

And now with the People Program class on "Listening to Good Music," with Caryl "Tiny" Barnes, I have had much joy. She's is great pianist and knows music so well, as well as being a good teacher. Together, we enter our second session, and plan to get our large class deeper into what constitutes good music and how to enjoy it: Classical, Jazz, Popular, Ragtime, Opera, Blues, whatever. Few things come close to Music and what the Muses bring to us.

## STORY 41: "BEAN," THE SKUNK

In my first year at St. Ben's Seminary, (1946), there were many new sensations to experience—I had never been away from home for any length of time, but I enjoyed my life there.

We carried many academic hours in our classes, especially Latin. Study was not difficult because we had Study Hall every evening for a couple of hours: we had no choice. Also, we studied French, History, English, Greek, Theology, and of course, Latin itself (St. Augustine's "Confessions," Virgil, Homer and his "Odyssey"). For someone who had had only one year of Latin in high school, it was a rather challenging prospect, but Fr. Augustine was a good teacher of "Three Years of Latin in One Year." So, Gene Lafleur, Les Prescott, and I plowed into it (and went on, years later, to be ordained priests together).

One evening shortly after I entered, something happened after supper in the yard near the refectory. A group of the seminarians (there were 400 of us on campus) flushed out a mother skunk and her young ones. Naturally, these city boys didn't quite get it—and the odor was present for everybody to put up with for the next few weeks. But in the confusion, as they threw sticks at the skunks, she became separated from her two children, who were badgered in the yard.

I saw my chance when the tiny skunks ran around and were scattered. I grabbed one of them, and put it away in my pocket. I knew that I had taken a chance, but there were many unusual pet animals among the students—squirrels which we trapped, flying squirrels, rabbits, (maybe snakes for all that I knew), and now a young skunk. I began to call him "Bean." I fed him milk with a medicine dropper and later on, table food as he grew. He was a good pet—very clean and cute, and I took good care of him.

I wrote my family about Bean. They were delighted and welcomed him. Daddy wrote that he knew a man who could "de-odorize him," he said. So, the next time my family visited, they were introduced to Bean, and they took him home for the surgery for me. It all went well—the job was done, and, for all we knew, all was well.

Bean was welcomed at home (of course, one of the Seminary Prefects later informed me that I could not keep him because of the obvious danger). At home, we had a cat called Mabel who ruled the roost. Mom fed Mabel and Bean together in separate dishes. This went on for several months, and, in the meantime, Bean grew to full stature. Daddy said it was so funny to see the reactions of people to a skunk running around our house. No mice or rats at all—Bean easily took care of that problem for us.

One evening, Mom fed the two as usual. When Mabel finished her food, she meandered over to Bean's dish and promptly ate it up. Bean didn't like that—he first stamped his front feet, and Mabel ate on, unconcerned; she completely ignored him. Another stamp, with no notice. And then chemical-biological warfare! Bean turned, lifted up his tail, and let us know that he had not been totally de-odorized—Mabel got it full in the face.

Mom told me later that Mabel froze, screamed, jumped high into the air, and then took off—and that's the last any of us saw of Mabel to this day! The odor and the memory would linger on.

Somehow later on, Bean either died or disappeared, quite probably he met his own "pretendu" and began a family of his own, without disturbance from any other pet. We lived in an area not far from the fields and woods back of New Roads where skunks were not unusual to be seen (or smelled).

It was obvious that the man who had done the de-odorizing did not do a complete job. But Bean was a very nice pet to have and to play with; this was the only instance of his dropping any more of his bombs on anyone. He was not as nice as a pet crow would have been—but I was never able to catch a crow, so I made do with Bean.

# STORY 42: The Sweetest Words in the English Language

As we grew up, both on St. Jude Street and at the house on the Morganza Highway, we had one and sometimes two cows—Alice, the first and best, and then Jane, her daughter. They were Jersey cows and gave us good, rich milk, cream, and butter. In fact, in high school, in the 4H Club, Alice was my project—we were friends.

Having cows meant that morning and evening, we had to milk them and take care of the calves, and we had to see about having them bred and getting their health checked regularly.

Milking the cow was not an onerous job, but, when it was cold and early in the morning before school, it was not the most pleasant chore; but it had to be done. "Va tire la vache!" ("Go milk the cow")—"OK, Mom, wait" brought about some scolding: "What? Don't tell me to wait, boy. What are you doing?" "I'm reading a book." "Un autre malheureau book!"

Milking had to take place in the barn where we kept the cows sheltered. On St. Jude, we would walk the cow during the day to a vacant lot, to chain her to a stob driven into the ground, or walk her to a pasture (usually that of Mr. Vitas Pourciau, back of the track, about a mile from home). At night, they stayed in the yard.

On the Morganza highway, the pasture was large enough for us to let them roam there and then bring them to the barn (which had been moved from St. Jude's—Daddy had built it with a stable, a corn-crib, with an upstairs where we kept the cow-feed, hay, and corn.) The cow-feed was cotton seed meal and cotton-seed hulls: we mixed the two together—the cows loved it, and it kept them nourished (as they nourished us with their rich milk). But it was part of the chore.

In the winter-time, especially at our present home, we had little shelter behind the barn and stable. (Of course, it got very muddy in and around the stable—and it was not all mud—if you know what I mean—it was knee-deep.) So, it meant boots, washing up and change of clothes—before school in the morning. And beforehand, we had to fix the feed for her to eat while we did the milking, in the stable out of the weather.

When we went to milk, we had to have the covered milk bucket with some warm water to wash the bag. Also, in the winter, we had to have some sort of salve or ointment for the bag, since they chapped easily. Sometimes Jane would have some discomfort and would kick when we began milking.

As we got into it, we had a stool to sit on, and we would get on the right side of the cow; extend a hand and push on the cow's hip and say, "Pied, Alice" and press so that she would move her leg back so that we could reach the teats and then settle in on the work. It didn't take very long—about 15 minutes for the actual milking: usually about a half-gallon.

And if there was a calf, it meant a problem—he was always hungry and felt that it was his civil right to get all that milk we were trying to steal from him. Sometimes, the cow could retain her milk so that we couldn't get it out. Once the calf came in, she'd let it go, but we had to fight the calf to another stall in the stable while we were milking only the two of the four teats. Afterwards, he could suck whatever was left. This went on until he was weaned, and he could eat feed or pasture.

As I mentioned, it meant a hassle, but it was worth it. In the winter mornings, sometimes we had enough milk, and Mom would speak the sweetest words in the English language: "Let the calf go with the cow—we have enough milk." O happy day. But we would be sure to milk in the evening to catch up.

Not only did this mean a happy kid—but also a happy calf, and he lapped it up and got fat on it.

## "Lemme Tell You a Story"

# STORY 43: What was he thinking?

Several years after we had completed our church, I was working in the office by myself one afternoon, when there came a knock at the door. Going to the door and opening it, I found myself looking at a man whom I vaguely remembered. Letting him in, I put out my hand—he took it and asked (without any hello or greeting), "A.J., do you know who I am? I'm your cousin, and I want you to do something for me."

With those words, I knew that I shouldn't have opened the door. He was dressed in work clothes—that was OK, but they weren't very clean: in fact, he looked scruffy. I recognized from the thick glasses someone whom I had known many years earlier, but whose path I had not crossed in over 25 years.

I greeted him, "Hello, Jamie; how are you? I haven't seen you in over 20 years. What can I do for you?" He carried a thick binder with pictures and drawings.

"I want you to sell my boat for me. I made it in Slidell, and I came for you to sell it for me—it's a good boat, all welded, 50 feet long with a diesel motor. You know a lot of people, and you can sell it easy—the people around here are rich." (Dismay.) "I want you to look over these plans and pictures I have here, and you can make a commission when you sell it." (More dismay.)

And then came the question from me—"How much?" His response blew me away—"I want $125,000 for it, but, if you sell it for more than that, it's OK. It's a good boat; I trawled with it, and it does work well. But I want to get rid of it so that I can build another one."

(Careful.) "Jamie, I don't know if you realize it, but I'm not in the business of selling boats. I'm a priest here, and my work is something entirely different." He answered, "I know that, but I thought that, since I need and I'm your cousin, you would do it for me. I know we haven't seen each other much for many years, but that doesn't matter. Will you do it for me?"

How to let him down gently? "Jamie, let me try to explain something to you. The people around here are not fishermen, even on weekends, and besides, I've got my hands full trying to be a priest for our families. Selling boats, and for that price, is not my line at all. Why don't you ask my brothers—you remember they have a welding and machine shop in New Roads, and that would be more in their line and not in mine. See them."

He really believed that, since I was his cousin, I would make an exception—he even offered to bring the boat to park in our parking space and show it off. He really thought that this would work.

So, he gathered up his folder and headed for the door. "Jamie, I'm sorry, but that wouldn't work—it's not in my line. By the way, what church do you go to?" No answer. And I opened the door for him as he left. Haven't heard or seen him since (that was over 20 years ago). I hope he has sold the boat and moved to greener pastures.

## STORY 44: You Mix the Army, Homesickness, Uncertainty, Mardi Gras, and What Do You Get?

It was 1961, and our Army Unit (the 159th Evacuation Hospital) had been mobilized to Ft. Sill, Oklahoma for how long we had no idea (because of the Berlin Wall Blockade). And it wasn't fun anymore. We had been a National Guard Unit at Jackson Barracks for years, Doctors, Nurses and Enlisted Men, meetings every week and summer camp at Ft. Polk. Then we were sent to this table-top place, with so much wind, dust, cold and heat, and it began to play on the nerves of the men.

First, they wrote to their congressmen, to no avail; then, to their governor back in Louisiana, again, to no avail. Then they got creative—they wrote to Johnny Carson on the "Tonight Show" which brought about some undesirable publicity. We were soundly warned to cease and desist, all of which made matters worse. What to do? We had a morale problem, and it was getting worse every day. Some AWOLs, and much grumbling. How to direct our energy into something constructive? "Chaplain, what can we create to bring up their spirits?"

Getting together with the men, most of whom were from New Orleans, it became evident that, even if they missed their "Yat food," what they missed even more was Carnival and all it meant to the City and its people. It began slowly, and then moved into logistics. A parade? No—too much difficulty having to argue with people who didn't understand. What about a Carnival Ball? Oh, maybe.

A band began to get together (we could borrow instruments from the Post Services), and started practicing heavily—some good musicians in the Unit. We needed not only a Dance Band, but also, being a Carnival Ball, you had to have a Jazz Band (to entertain the King and Queen and their Court). What about costumes for the Krewe? Not on this Post. Well, what about borrowing some from home? Oh, it might work: we have many of our people who were members of the Krewes—in St. Bernard, New Orleans, and across the Lake.

It all began to fall into place—the Colonel said, "OK, try it and see; it just might work." And somehow more and more people began to work with decorations; music was purchased; costumes began to arrive from home and adjusted. And the spirit began to grow after Christmas.

There are few places which are as lonely and deserted as an Army Post for Thanksgiving, and especially for Christmas. Worship services, Masses and Sacraments at the Post Chapels were held with a direction toward what we hoped would be a little taste of "home away from home." But we weren't sure.

The dance band began to sound quite good—after all, we wouldn't have to play for more than an hour. But the Jazz Band was something else. Instruments we picked up—it would have to have a "wash-tub" bass; I could tune my banjo like a ukulele and it would work; we got drums for our drummer—we had a hot trumpet player who had his own horn, as did the clarinet and the trombone. All getting enthused, especially after we made the white "boater straw hats" out of cardboard, with the red striped jackets sewn and worn: class.

We would be called the "Dixieland Dukes of Caduceus"—now that's hot and we loved it. We would entertain the King, Queen, and their Court after they were seated and presented, all with their robes, gowns, plumes (and yes, even the beads were thrown!)

People we never dreamed who would get involved began to help out. Hey, what about some tumblers to entertain the Court? OK, do we have anyone to do that? Yes, one of the wives does some tumbling and dancing—she can train some of the girls to do it. Larry's wife, Kay, is very good and she will love it.

Programs were printed, food was prepared, and then the date began to get closer. The complaining began to subside "How do you spell "Caduceus"—you know, that "snake on a stick, the emblem of the Medical Corps"?

Our theme song was the most logical one in the world—"Do You Know What It Means to Miss New Orleans?" And we knew.

Came the night of the Ball, and it was a marvelous event. The Officers wore their dress uniforms; everyone put on his and her best manners, and it went off without a hitch. Compliments replaced complaints. In fact, there were commendation medals earned by a few people, but the most important fact was that the Unit was able to continue running the Hospital at Fr. Sill until we were mustered out in the Fall of that year, with a good report. And that Carnival Ball was truly fun and the highlight of that year.

## STORY 45: A PUZZLEMENT: What to do?

Vietnamese people began to arrive in our community in 1975 to live in Woodland Estates—elderly, young, weary, scared, pitiful. They needed medical attention (even to body lice!), clothes, housing, interpreters, transportation, jobs, and food stamps. And a dedicated group of people from our surrounding churches jumped right in to help them. It was a beautiful sight—these poor people brought with them little guidance or leadership, and, within a short period of time, Good Samaritans put them under their wings.

People from St. Philip' s Episcopal, St. Stephen's Lutheran, Woodland Presbyterian, Algiers Methodist, and Holy Spirit Catholic, plus the nuns from Our Lady of Holy Cross Convent became their shepherds. Morning, noon, and night the calls went out from the nurses among us aimed at their medical needs; also, the public health Hospital and Catholic Charities gave time, instruction, and guidance to help them. There were about 1,800 Vietnamese, and most of them in our area were Catholics, very devout.

At the time, our parish was using the beautiful chapel at Our Lady of Holy Cross College for Masses and gatherings. Also, alas, I was severely ill (and taking massive doses of Prednisone for an auto-allergic illness, called Pemphigus) but kept going anyway.

One Sunday, shortly after they arrived among us, I began to notice that, as devout as they were, many were not receiving

Holy Communion, which made me curious. So, I consulted with Mr. Duke, a young translator among them. "Why aren't those people—who are great praying Catholics—not receiving the Eucharist? They should be, I suspect." His answer: "Father, it's been months since they've been able to go to Confession—the Sacrament of Reconciliation. We have so few priests among the group who could hear their confession."

So I took this problem to a priest friend who knows his Canon law, and he made it clear to me that this was a good situation for me to give them sacramental absolution; General Absolution, which is usual under extreme conditions, such as chaplains in the service preparing their men for battle in adverse conditions. "OK, I think I'm going to try it—never done it before: there's always a first time."

The next Sunday, before we began the Mass (although the Vietnamese elders had already been chanting their prayers for an hour, in their sing-song fashion, from early morning—I thought they probably said every prayer they knew, and that was a lot!), I asked Mr. Duke to have his people stay in their pews.

And then I explained that, knowing that they had not been to the Sacraments for months, I could give them general absolution—I would pray the ritual for them, and he would translate. So it went. I was careful, trying hard to be kind and gentle. They were and are a beautiful people. It was very solemn—they were right with it.

After we finished, I was so touched. As they left the Holy Cross Chapel, they sang a beautiful hymn on their way home. And I was so gratified—we do have those "Aha!" moments frequently in the priesthood where it all falls into place, and it all is clearly so worthwhile.

From that time on, the whole group was at Communion every time, and I felt as if I had had a "coup" from Jesus our

Shepherd. I continued saying Mass for them on Tuesdays in an apartment in Woodland Estates. And on Sundays, for ten years they used the St. Philip Church and Holy Spirit Church, until they built their own church with their own priest, Fr. Joseph Tue. He became a good friend and spent 27 years among those people before being transferred to the St. Agnes Vietnamese church in Marrero. Vietnamese people continue to attend our church, especially now that they can come to Mass with their family—at their church, the "boys sit on the right, and the girls sit the left." And I like having them here—they've been a welcome gift to our Archdiocese and our city.

## STORY 46: Strange and Different

It is said that the more we're alike, the more we are different. And so it is with priests. I am now in my 55th year of Priesthood, and when I think of it, I marvel at how rich our experience is. Funny, and different.

Yesterday, we priests honored Archbishop Hughes who is now retiring and awaiting the arrival of Archbishop Greg Aymond, who will be elevated on August 20, '09. A luncheon was scheduled at an "ultra restaurant," on Tchoupitoulas Street. Fr. Jerry Stapleton and I drove together and finally found the place—priests were all hurrying in to be on time. Black clerical suits, some with "bishop chains," gathered and entered the building; quite proper.

After Jerry and I parked, we walked the three blocks and felt the hot busy day as we slowly approached the hotel from across the street. Coming to a corner, we stopped, and a man hurriedly walked past us. He was rushing past us, and he turned and called out, "Hello, Allen. Hi, Jerry." And I responded, "Hello, Jim, glad to see you!" He kept going.

Carrying a blue clerical shirt, he moved past us when we crossed the street and came to the hotel door. I could see Jim standing at the curb removing his shirt. I suspected that he dumped his old shirt. We went in, and, when we reached the dining room, I marveled to see Jim, now wearing his blue shirt, sitting at a table (where the Monsignors surely were going to give him the facts of life about clerical dress). Obviously, he wore that shirt so that he would not be barred by the waiters from participating with all those black suits! But he was now in with us all, among friends.

Jim was ordained a priest many years ago and is thought to be one of the best well-read priests in the Archdiocese. Over time, he's been assigned to many parishes and is not too worried about his attire (which was such an important idea among us oldsters.) It's been a sort of mantra with some pastors. I'm tempted these days to agree with them; even though we no longer like to have a uniform on with the idea of "Why do we have to advertise that we are priests?" It invites some hooligan or a drunk to holler out to us, as I've experienced it, "Hey, Father, don't play with little boys, you hear?"

Those feelings get twisted into an odd thought. Since the Vatican Council, there has been a relaxing of the strict obligation to always be wearing a Roman collar or the cassock. I admire Jim for his service in the Diocese, even if we don't see each other very often: he probably lives a life of poverty and of prayer, which makes my own efforts seem stuffy and something for me to consider. We are living in a different time: and I pray for us priests. We are living in "new paradigms," someone said. What an interesting life we lead.

# STORY 47: "Ask and you shall receive . . ." (Luke's Gospel, 11:9)

It's interesting how, sometimes when we're busy thinking about or doing something else, a thought comes to mind which opens the way into many other facets of our memories. Today, a Saturday, I was at prayer in the church, getting ready for the evening Mass, and, having talked with my younger brother, Jerry, I recalled an incident which happened when I was 5 or so, and he was 2. The family was struggling—Daddy worked on the levee with a mule and scraper.

We lived in Waterloo, 15 miles back of New Roads, a very deserted area, along the Mississippi levee, surrounded by cows in their pastures—the houses, poor as they were, were almost a mile apart. My Godmother and her family lived along the same road, and we visited quite often and shared our food and company. Today, that area is one of the exclusive gated communities in Pointe Coupee parish.

Mom and Marain had noticed that the owner of the cattle around us regularly would come to visit a black family, miles past us—he was engaged in an affair with one of the black women. They had agreed that, when Mr. M would drive by in his Model T, they would stop him and talk to him.

Sure enough, one day around noon, Mr. M was headed down the dusty road toward his destination. Mom, with Jerry and me, waved him down. He stopped, unsure what that was about (but, I suspect that he feared being found out and gossip spread—we saw him at church where he was well-thought of). He got out of the car and approached us.

Mom greeted him, and, without hesitation, she asked him, "Mr. M, we noticed that you have a momma cow who has lost her calf just the last few days. She keeps mooing and moving around, searching for her calf. She has a nice bag and looks like she has a lot of milk. But if she's not milked, she will go dry. Would you mind or have any objection if we milked her? We need that milk bad."

I'm standing there, taking it all in. And of course, I had to say something. I chimed in, "Mr. M, we need that milk: you see that little boy there? That's my little brother. He's hungry and so skinny that when he poo-poos, all that comes out is worms!" Gritty, but effective.

Mr. M, stammered, and, hurriedly, he said, "Yes, you can have the cow's milk. But remember, as you milk her, that she's still my cow." And he drove off, certainly not aware of where that interchange would go. We have been grateful to that man and recall his cow and how much that meant to us in our depression-era poverty.

Later on, Daddy began a blacksmith shop in town, and we moved to Red Stick street where I entered school, and life went on always upward. God has been good to us.

Jesus said, "Ask and you will receive; seek and you shall find." How true that was. Jerry and I have laughed about that incident, many times.

## STORY 48: "One never knows what he will find . . ."

Quite frequently, we do not know what we're dealing with in priestly ministry. And, as pastor, I have had to become very involved in many marriages and families that I encounter. So much of that involves outreach to people who are into invalid marriages and people who want to "bless their marriage."

There was a family in our parish, years ago, whose mother was gravely ill at Charity Hospital. I had already begun the canonical process to bless the marriage of this mother and her husband. After the process was complete, I got word from the family that the mother was close to dying. Would we be able to bless the marriage soon? I was so glad to do it especially with the family and their seven children present near her bed in the ward.

When I entered her ward, I saw before me what I had not expected: the mother was still in bed, dressed with a veil, and the husband, in tie and coat, surrounded by the children and her mother, all dressed up. They had spread a sheet on the bed, covering the blanket, as she sat up, with her husband standing at her side and holding her hand.

As solemnly as I could, I led us into the instructions for the Sacrament of Marriage and came to the vows: "Will you? Yes, I will"; "Will you, Yes, I will." We completed the ceremony and came to the solemn blessing. I wished them well, congratulated them, and moved to the door to go back to the rectory to record the wedding in the register.

When I got to the door out of the ward, I turned to see the joy and relief of the family. Then I watched as the mother reached over and took off the sheet which had been covering the bed and saw that, while it was covering the bed, it revealed that the "bride," throughout the ceremony, was sitting on a bed pan! They lay her down again in the bed. If I had known that, what would that have mattered anyway?

How solemn we are, but still the human is so present, and that's part of what makes the priesthood so interesting and so human. I encounter that beauty so frequently—it makes my life so full of humor and joy.

## STORY 49: Grandpa's heritage

Because my grandparents seemed to live so far from us, we didn't know a lot about them. My dad's parents lived in Mansura, 60 miles away, and, at the time, that seemed far away from New Roads.

In 1982, after my grandfather passed away, their ten children gathered for the dividing of their "nest-egg," which he had often spoken of: he told his children that they would be rich! My dad had already been dead about twenty years, so my brother Jerry and Mom were present for that special occasion, to represent Daddy with the family. Since I was stationed near New Orleans at the time, I only heard about it all afterwards.

It seems that, when they began to put away their savings stash in the mattress (it was during the Great Depression), many of the banks had failed, and there was much fear that all the other banks would fail. Also, I don't think that Grandpa, a farmer, paid too much income tax or Social Security, even if they were not as poor as we were.

My brother told me that first they hid it in the mattress, and, when that became a problem, they looked for another place where people would not expect it to be hidden. It appears that they decided to put it into the ground, deeply planted, back of the back yard outhouse (which was always as immaculately scrubbed as I've ever seen one). And this lasted for several years. But the fear persisted.

So, Grandpa decided to bury it down the well, which itself was so well kept and guarded. He put it into the wall of the well (how he did that, I have no idea), several feet underground. And that, too, lasted several years. But move it again he did.

Then, he hit upon THE place which would not only be safe from discovery, but it would be close enough so that he could keep watch and guard his secret. He decided to dig under the fire-bricks of his fireplace. Again, it was a couple of feet below the fire-bed where the heat would not affect the pile, and no one would suspect. And there it remained for more years than the other places. Until, first Grandma died and a few years later Grandpa joined her.

I bring up this story not to ridicule them or criticize all these arrangements, but to bring to our attention how much the atmosphere then is no longer that of our daily lives and living. When the family divided the inheritance and I received my share, it was a nice bundle, and I received it with gratitude.

Really, I had given up the idea that, as the family increased, my share would be more than only a few dollars. But it was a nice gift from my grandparents, who left me not only my DNA, but also enough to move me to do a story about it.

## STORY 50: World War II—A High School Story

It was 1942, and our country was at war. In New Roads, we were unaware of so much reality happening around us; we knew rationing (the stamps, the "A" sticker on the car's windshield—the items which were no longer available to us). We were at the edge of poverty (but we were also unaware of that fact), and the draft was in place (we played in the high school band for every group of men called up to enter the service on a regular basis).

We knew the urgency of what President Franklin D. Roosevelt called "the day of infamy," the attack on Pearl Harbor. I was a sophomore in high school; at the time, one graduated from $11^{th}$ grade at St. Joseph Academy and its sister (public school), Poydras High. It was a good life: a small southern town of about 2,500 families clustered around False River, untouched by integration or any real awareness of what the rest of the world was experiencing, even in the nearby city of Baton Rouge.

We were part of different drives to help the war effort—scrap metal drives, paper drives, war-bond drives, prayers for the success and return of our hometown servicemen. Among these was the plan for a "Victory Garden" by our school. It was only a couple of blocks away from the school grounds, behind the Masonic Hall.

The plot we were preparing was tilled by hand by us and divided into rows for the various vegetables we would plant, weed, and water. Rows of tomatoes, corn, peppers, egg plants, and cucumbers. My two rows of corn had my care and concern; all of this was under the supervision of our teachers, most of whom were Sisters of St. Joseph. We worked there on our own time and were supervised rather loosely.

One day after the garden began to grow, I was watching my corn, about a foot high, and saw John H walking into the garden rows and mashing down my corn plants. I came to him and fussed, "Don't do that, John! That's my corn and you're ruining the row!" He swore at me and kicked a couple of the corn plants. "I don't care—this whole garden business is a bunch of foolishness. I'm not going to waste my damned time—you're a fool to do all this." So, I pushed him off my corn row. Naturally, he pushed me back, and it became a pushing contest.

And the more the pushing went, the angrier we both became. Finally (and all of this took place among the rows and my nice corn), he grabbed me and got his arm around my neck, choking me. I yelled, "Now quit that. You don't fight fair!" Nothing. So, desperation set in—I was gasping for breath. This called for drastic measures.

Dragged around, I swung my right fist and aimed for the groin. And succeeded—I hit with all that I had, and he screamed, "You don't fight fair. And you hurt me, you SOB!" But he let me go and bent double in pain. Oh, that was sweet. Ruined a lot of my corn plants, but that didn't matter anymore. All the while, nobody else was in the garden—I couldn't even brag about my first and only fight. To me, it was a real victory Victory Garden. God bless John H.

# STORY 51: "The Difficult"

As I look back on my life, I find many areas which have made my life cumbersome. And as I reflect upon these areas, the question arises: "Why should this give me trouble or grief"? There is the possibility of the reason being shyness ("Me, shy?"); or inexperience ("Well, it could be"); or the fear of ridicule ("Could be, too"); or, some sort of insecurity, something back in my past which made me specially sensitive to having to lead a discussion, or chairing a meeting of peers. Perhaps it's because I don't want to look incompetent to the "boys." Vanity?

Up until I was elected president of the St. Ben's Seminary Alumni association, I had never chaired a meeting even if I had attended myriads of them. I had never studied Robert's Rules of Order and did not bother about it when someone else showed knowledge and competence in parliamentary procedure. I was loath to handle a gavel, or call for a vote, or pass a motion.

When I became president, I really leaned on others to help me, and it went very well, and I was re-elected. (I had a lot of experience in being secretary of many groups—I typed well, and took good notes, all of which made me a potential for election as president. And so it happened.)

But when it happened that I was elected Dean of the Algiers-Plaquemines Deanery, with its 10 parishes and schools, I realized that I would have to plan, prepare, and conduct our priests/deacons' meetings, and I began to sweat. (I should say at this juncture that the priest I replaced as Dean was one who was at ease with this job and didn't want to let it go, although his tenure was over.

The very first meeting was a disaster: it was at All Saints Church on Teche Street. I had all my hand-outs, plans, arrangements, and agenda set up. But my boy had a priest friend of his with him, who also was adept at making fun of others. I was nervous, and they didn't care. And they poured it on, until finally, I had enough, and I told my boy, "Look, you're being obstructive, and you offend me!" That toned the stuff down, but it would emerge greatly in future meetings. I realized that I had to protect my parish from being absorbed by the neighboring parish, and I did so, with my guard always up in vigilance.

I concentrated on being calm and more relaxed as I continued for three successive terms as Dean. I realized that my nemesis would be looking over my shoulder, correcting and reproving me whenever he could, and doing it publicly, with my embarrassment. The discussions were important: we were concentrating on plans and future-vision which had to do with Catholic Life 2000 (now the basis of so much question and distress in the Archdiocese).

I completed my three terms and was so pleased when someone else was elected Dean (even if he lasted only nine months because of an accusation of impropriety with children.) And I continue asking myself why I had so much turmoil: I now have no problem in presiding, both at the Eucharist and all the meetings which ministry requires of me and us. God is good.

## STORY 52: Listening and What It Takes

How important it is for a priest/pastor to really listen to others. I've always taken so seriously my relating to others, especially when someone needed and wanted counseling. To look into someone's soul, thoughts, plans, and admissions is a privilege only a few have given to them. This is not an easy skill to have: it must be reflected upon, practiced, learned, and constantly exercised.

It occurs to me, these latter years, how it is much more difficult to listen than it used to be in the past. Not because there is a lack of interest or one becoming "an introvert," but rather the hearing becomes more and more dependent upon the dreaded HEARING AID. (*#?!!—it!)

Having one ear hearing normally, the other gets attention with its hearing aid—on what side does one want to be so that he will hear and be able to listen? And why is it that people (especially women) talk so fast these days? The words, words, words all tumble out in a constant pattern without even having a pause between them. Perhaps we might be trying too hard. Was she trying to say "Patter," and what I understood was "Tatter"? Did she say, "Prostrate," and I understood "Prostate"? This never happened before: and it's quite a difference.

How satisfying it is when people ask us to listen to them, and, in their grief or anger, we can help them achieve a peaceful state of mind, as they pour it all out to look at their situation from an outside viewpoint.

What trust that takes—the risk people take in exposing themselves to being viewed and perhaps judged something else besides mature, level, and balanced. The gift that people place in our hearts and hands when they entrust to us their innermost secret of hurt, fear, anger and upset, or worse, indecision: "I just don't know what to do—can you help me?"

Just hearing is not all there is to it—to listen, to enter into their pain, fear, anger, or their joy, is such a privilege. So many hear but do not LISTEN—to shut out any distraction and give that person our whole attention, experience, skill and desire to help them. And know what it is to have found a listening heart—"once you have found a listening and understanding heart, you have found a treasure: he is like a wall of brass, a tower of iron," and with his help you can go on. You have found a little place of God in your midst, holy ground. God somehow has now been made present to you—be grateful.

# STORY 53: "I WISH I HAD LISTENED . . ."

After I was ordained a priest, I had a good and pleasant assignment with two other priests. lasting for three years. I was the low man on the totem pole, and Bill, my fellow assistant pastor, was a good priest who took me under his wing and really helped me learn and grow. He had been assigned there a year before I arrived. He was a prayerful man, a lover of good music, easy to be with, and very pastoral although sometimes I found him putting on airs when he was with people who didn't live in the Ninth Ward at Our Lady Star of the Sea parish, on St. Roch Park. We were part of the "downtown trash" of the time.

For the first year and a half, we lived in an old rectory which had two floors. The bottom floor was dingy—and was where the two of us assistants each had a room with a bathroom we shared between us. The ceilings were quite low and old. In fact, when I had been there for a year and a half, we moved to a temporary rectory while a new one was built in the same address.

The pastor's niece was the housekeeper with her wet-back Mexican husband and her dog who had the run of the upstairs part of the house. She had been the bane of the two assistants who had been there before us. Spying for her uncle and reporting to him on us about what she knew he didn't want us to do. He didn't do a lot of the pastoral work and had little real contact with the people of the parish, even though he was easy enough to get along with. But he was quite slow to spend for anything other than on food, about which he was very particular. I really had little real human contact with him, except to make certain that I didn't violate the regulations which I heard he had made and which were extended to me by my fellow-assistant and the housekeeper.

After I had been installed there several months, I realized that Bill, my fellow assistant, had almost daily urged me,

"Now, Man, I'm so glad you don't smoke—I don't think that our arrangement could last if you did. Remember, I have the air-conditioner in my room and only allow you to get the cool from it." And I just sloughed it off—after all, I was an adult and didn't want someone to invade my preferences, other than those whose authority I had to observe. In those days, the major virtue was obedience, and the blinder it was, the better. But smoking was a common thing.

Having heard those warning words so many times, my arrogance began to grow and I refused to listen. My dad smoked, as did my brother as well. I tried it a few times, and coughed and choked, but once one got used to it, it wasn't so bad—in fact, it was enjoyable in a different way. After all, the cigarette was a companion, a play-toy, something to play with, ( and perhaps a connection with my mother's breast) and the nicotine was all right. That was okay since I knew I would not let myself become addicted. Foolish thing. I didn't smoke cigars, couldn't take a pipe, and only puffed on less than a pack a day of Lucky Strikes. I didn't smoke in my room, but only in my office—we had no air-conditioning in the upstairs.

Finally, once I realized smoking had become a part of my life, it was too late. I was hooked. This went on for about ten years, until our rectory in my later assignment in Chauvin burned down. It was then that I realized that I wasn't smoking the cigarettes, but I was smoking the habit, without enjoyment. And it had to end if I made up my mind.

So, I looked ahead to the days afterwards, when our school would finish the Visitation by the Southern Association of Schools and Colleges in October. As we prepared for that, I then decided that I would quit. Not easy, but I did it, cold turkey. And since then, I haven't had another puff, thank God. But if only I had listened to Bill, I would have not been so burdened.

# STORY 54: SCARED

It was 1945; the war was still going on, and I was all of 15 years old. To improve their law enforcement, the Pointe Coupee Parish Sheriff's office acquired a radio system for all their deputies to communicate throughout the parish. It was a big deal. My dad had a welding and machine shop, and he was hired by Mr. Jack to install the radio antenna tower on the roof of the jail in New Roads. The tower was in five 15 foot segments to total 65 feet above the three-story Sheriff's office, a total of about 150 feet in the air.

The first step was to dig four holes in the flat concrete roof, which I did, using a star-drill and hammer (my hands were so sore from the pounding that for two days afterwards, I couldn't hold anything). We would bolt down the base of the tower and, with cables, hold it in place in safe efficiency. The first section, about 15 feet long, was bolted onto the base plate, and the next segments would be bolted to the first as the tower got taller. We were to install and then climb each section—Mr. Jack to bolt them together, Daddy to guide the next section into place with him. All of us had safety-belts to hold us to the triangular steel tower.

I would be the lowest man on the tower to pull on the rope to lift each of the next sections into place and bring up the "coaxial cable" to be connected. This rope was attached to a pulley on the end of a heavy pipe called a gym-pole which would be secured to the topmost section and then the next section from down below would be lifted by rope into place and secured.

As we moved higher and higher with each section into place, the guy-wire cables were secured to hold our weight in safety. I also noted that, after the third section was in place, from that height, I could see far above the courthouse tower even to the other side of False River. And I felt safe: we took all precautions and moved deliberately so as not to endanger ourselves or others. It was all going smoothly, and we were pleased with our progress. Visitors from the Sheriff's Office came by frequently to inspect our progress and sometimes brought us soft drinks. We had been at work on it for at least two weeks.

I really felt as if I was holding up my part as a man should. But then somehow, we had a mishap. After the fourth section was secured and bolted, 60 feet up, the two men above me raised the gym-pole to put it into place so as to lift the next final section. I heard my dad call out, "Look out, the gym-pole has slipped!" When I did look, I saw that this 15 foot heavy pole was swinging to come down and hit the tower across from where I was hanging on! And all I could do was to watch it breathlessly and hold on.

It slammed right across from me with a loud clatter, jarring the whole tower. Now, I was scared. I mean SCARED. Spitless. And my dad came through: he told me, "Jay, hold on, you hear me? Don't look down, boy—just look at me and don't move!" Good advice, because at that moment, I had had enough—I wanted to go home and be anywhere else except up there in the air hanging onto a strap which held me to that tower in the sky. If it had hit me, it would have given me a giant headache at the least and spoiled the whole morning.

Luckily, we completed the job we had to do, and I didn't have to climb there anymore. But that day, I knew what fear was, and I was fortunate that no one was injured or worse. And that tower is still there, in operation.

## STORY 55: "Un Coeur Casse'?"

Her name was Laura, a girl from Laplace who played the bassoon in the Parish Band at Pointe Coupee Band Camp in 1945. Daily, for two weeks, we practiced music for hours a day, and I got interested in her. She was a good musician but very shy and quiet.

The Band had some social outings, and we went out together a few times. By the time that Band Camp was over, I was smitten. Her returning home to Laplace afterwards was uneventful, and I had gotten through her departure with only a photo of her. I hid it in the only secure place I could think of: at the bottom of the drawer in the dresser in my room. Naturally, my little brother found it and told Mom, and she of course had to tell everybody about me and my girl.

I missed her, and I was mortified—"A. J.'s got a girl—"Une Dagotte"—"Ha, Ha—L'Amour!", "Puppy-foot love, Ha, Ha!" I even thought, one time, that I had seen her on a train passing through. Those were the words of the song "Laura," popular at that time. But that faded after several weeks. Some love affair.

I graduated from high school the next year and forgot about all this. Entering the seminary that same year, I graduated from junior college, and entered the major seminary, and, after six years, was ordained a priest. This brought in a three-year appointment in one parish and another for four years. After several years, one Sunday afternoon, I conducted a pre-marital class for Pre-Cana couples at Our Lady of Mount Carmel.

In the group, I spied a familiar face—Laura with her fiancé. It was a joyful meeting. I met her fiancé, and we had a chance to talk. After the conference, we walked a little, and I told her, "You know, Laura, you're the reason I am a priest today."

She stopped walking and, in a very confident voice, spoke some immortal amorous words which were emblazoned on my heart: "I'm sorry to tell you, I think you're nice, but I think you're full of bull!"

Sic transit gloria mundi.

# STORY 56: SOMETHING LOST

I have found, in the years that we have been together in our Storytelling class, that sometimes in our narratives, we are into revealing feelings, incidents, or attitudes about ourselves that we bring out to other people but are not completely comfortable in revealing. For an extrovert who is not usually shy enough, this may sound odd. But my narrative about the loss of something precious to me impels me to go into feelings and admission of behavior which I have never processed enough, and which I now regret. And that's why the loss has touched me.

My story is about a classmate named Mack, who was a very good friend of mine, perhaps my best friend at one time. We were both included in the special seminary class, which was faced with the challenge of jumping a couple of years of class study. We were both Cajuns who spoke French at home—country boys, also pretty good athletes, and serious about studying for the priesthood at the college level. Mack was admired and referred to as being "solid," which meant he was a good friend to have: smart, strong, and devout, even if his singing capacity was nil: it didn't mean the same to him as it did to me.

When we were chosen to this new avenue of study, it meant a lot more study and classwork, especially while we were home during the summer of 1947. (I had been in the seminary only one year.) Mack approached me one day and made this proposal: "You and I are very much alike—we care deeply about the same things. So, consider this: let's work together in this challenge we are into—like two mules who need to pull together and combine our strengths to pull the plow of this school business, and, in the process, help each of us to do well. Our prayer, our play, our classwork, let's pool it, and we'll make a good team, I think." I was pleased that he had chosen me to help support him and "make a good team with him."

And so it happened. Our daily work, our prayer, our seminary activities were made much smoother for both of us this way. We discussed the problems we faced, and it was good to have somebody who understood where we were coming from and who was open to entering into another's life to pool our strengths. The seminary framework frowned upon "particular friendships," so we were conscious that we not cut anyone else out of our activities. But I think that other students referred to us as good friends, but nothing more than that. There were some others whose insulated friendships were frowned upon and dangerous—ours was not. It was healthy.

We got through sixth class ($2^{nd}$ year college) and graduated together with the twelve classmates a couple of years ahead of what had been our class, to enter Notre Dame Seminary in 1948. Regularly, Mack and I discussed our lives, our prayer, our study, our families, and life itself. It was good. We seldom had disagreements, and those were not serious. I did note, however, that Mack was much more serious than I was. He didn't like "playing around"—the usual childish behavior of boys in school, and he made no bones about that. Looking back at it, this was possibly the only chink in the armor of our friendship, and I don't think that I gave it the attention I should have. And I regret that today, 62 years later.

We had duties for which we were responsible in the housekeeping at the seminary. I was sacristan for two years. Mack was bell-ringer and mailman. And this is where the something precious was lost. After lunch one day, Mack was distributing the mail in the Rec room; I was standing in front of him as he called out the names and handed out the letters. I made some sort of remark (I think, with no malice) and grabbed his cassock and pulled the buttons open. Without a break, he back-handed me across the mouth, without a word.

Surprised and hurt, I backed away and left the room. A bystander asked me, "Did that bastard just slap you?" And this began the loss. Time did not help it—we no longer walked together after meals as we had been doing. And I found that I was not ready to re-enter our friendship. Somehow, I felt that he had violated our closeness and done something I found hard to forgive and get past. BUT WE NEVER EVEN TRIED TO DISCUSS IT: neither he nor I. It was not the same. And I still mourn for that loss. Possibly, there may have been something else involved that was happening to Mack of which I was unaware. I'll never know.

Mack left the seminary several months later. Eventually I heard that he had married and had at least one son and died several years ago in Bunkie. But never a word from him, nor a word to him from me. And I wonder about how we can luck into something precious, and how, without thinking, we can not only throw it away, but never seek to retrieve it. "There are none so blind . . ."

I have thought about that event in my life many times and still carry guilt and regret about it all, as I'm sure he did, too. Was I wrong? Yes, I was. What I can't get is why that slap had to be so important.

But now, it's probably only the thoughts of an aging man about past years and its joys and woes. There have been many of each (the joys and the woes, that is), but this loss has been irretrievable, and all I can do is regret it and pray for his memory. He was a good friend.

## STORY 57: "The Fragrance of Wooden Matches and Coal Smoke"

There are two things that bring back strong memories for me! One is the smell of a wooden match when scratched, and the other is the smoke from a coal fire.

While I was in grammar school, I regularly went to my dad's blacksmith shop to help out. It had a dirt floor, and the forge was where I "worked"—I lighted the fire so that he could beat plow-points for the farmers in the area. Today, dad's shop would weld an edge on the plows and make them almost impervious to wear as they plowed in the fields. But at that time, they had to be heated and beaten on an anvil, which my daddy did. My job, after the fire was going in the forge, was to turn the handle of the blower to supply oxygen to the fire and make it even hotter and better able for the iron plow-points to be beaten.

When I got to the shop, my first job was to light the fire. With my pocketknife, I would cut the kindling, usually cypress shavings; I would bunch them in the forge and light them. Once the fire was going, I would add coal to make a very hot fire. That smoke was supposed to go up and out the vent above the forge, but, of course, it surrounded us in the shop. It was not a pleasant odor (as the smell of the match was not bad), but it would stop up my sinuses and "stay there" for the rest of the day. An unforgettable aroma.

But I was pleased that I could do something for my dad, and so, for the family (after all, I was the oldest son and was responsible to do my part).

So, ever since that time, every time I smell a struck match, the memories come back. For example, Dad's song was "Stardust," which came out in 1939 and was one of the most recorded by Hoagy Carmichael: "Sometimes I wonder why I spend the lonely night . . ." While he worked, Dad hummed and whistled that tune, and it carries a heavy reminder for me.

And, as for the coal smoke (although it isn't very often that I run into that smell), even if unpleasant, it still carries me back to those days (before and during World War II). They were good days, and I prize them.

# STORY 58: A Different Mother's Day

As the priest great-uncle of a new baby in the family, I was asked by Aimee to baptize her new daughter. Aimee is the youngest daughter of Butchie and Christie, he the oldest of my brother's sons and Christie his wife, now in her third year of ALS (known as "Lou Gehrig's Disease").

I have been very close to this family. When Aimee called me to ask if I could baptize her little Kylie Christine, I was honored. I live so far away that I seldom see them in my short visits home. But what stopped me in my tracks when she asked about baptism was that she asked if it would be possible for me to baptize Kylie at the foot of her mother's bed at her parents' home on Mother's Day. In that way her mother could participate in the baptism even if unable to move, or talk, or react with whatever is happening around her. She is present and nothing else. Furthermore, Aimee had discussed this event with her pastor and gotten his permission to do this.

So, after my second Mass at Holy Spirit, I headed toward home through Baton Rouge, and, in a little more than two hours, I was in New Roads, home at my brother's, the father of Butchie. We had dinner together, and, frankly, I was a quite apprehensive—I so wanted not to break down in tears before the whole group—that usually is so contagious and would make things awkward for all.

When we arrived at Christie's, there was a nice group there for the occasion, all of whom were now veterans of caring for Christie in her progressive path from awareness of ALS to the more intimate, day-in and day-out of having to do everything for her. Their living room/sickroom now held her hospital bed, a few chairs, plus the wheel-chair in the corner. Also, there were little Kylie's sister of 4 and her cousin Mason who were everywhere at once. How very natural in spite of the illness so obviously present to all. And since it was Mother's Day, there was some festivity—food prepared, a beautiful Mother's

Day cake, and a couple of large balloons all proclaiming the occasion. Christie was beautiful, as was the baby.

The baptism went smoothly (except for the pouring of the baptismal water when ole Kylie reacted to the water and got baptized in the eyes! But not a cry, or a peep from her: a lovely child with her grandmother's blue eyes and blond hair). After all the pictures were taken of all the family and youngsters, I had the opportunity of observing a sort of "Charades in reverse."

In the past when I visited, I was able to slowly communicate with Christie through her "Dyna-Vox," an electronic device which she operated with her eyes as it printed and spoke out what she spelled out by blinking her eyes. Today it was in the corner.

Instead, I watched Aimee come to sit at her Mom's bedside and have a strange sort of conversation with her. Christie had a question to ask Aimee who held a small poster on which was the alphabet and other written "tools" Butchie had rigged for them to be able to "talk." I watched Aimee hold the poster and point to one or other of the letters and spell them out as Christie identified the letters she wanted spelled out with her eyes. And Aimee then spoke the word Christie wanted said, and the question answered. Slow, deliberate, careful they were, until they understood her question. All she could move were her eyes: one blink, "yes," and two blinks, "no." All of it so frustrating to all of them because she had been such a vivacious nurse and mother only a couple of years before. But also a very evident strong patience and solicitude for her and her inclusion in the occasion.

Also, however, there was not a drop of tears or deploring the obvious situation. It was a beautiful experience to witness and be a part of. I would not have missed it for the world. Caring, urging, gentleness, and kindness: what beauty—all on Mother's Day.

# STORY 59: "A HOME-MADE SURPRISE ATTACK"

It was a nice spring day, and I was at the grocery store, waiting in line to check my loaded basket out. Behind me was a line of people and their filled baskets waiting for me to finish. As I stood there, I noticed that at the other three registers, large lines were also waiting. "What's the problem, Miss?" "The computers are down, and the registers are all stalled." So, we do what is the most difficult thing for us to do—just hunker down and w-a-i-t.

After about 20 minutes, I asked the clerk, "Miss, may I write you a check?" "Yes, sir, but I will need some identification—your driver's license." When I showed it, she looked at it and casually informed me, "Sir, your driver's license is expired!" "What? It can't be—I've shown this license to at least a dozen doctors' offices and they all approved it." Then I looked and saw that it was so true!!! And thus began a saga. I paid for the groceries with cash and left.

Going to the driver's license bureau office, I found a couple of dozen people who were already there, waiting. After waiting for an hour and a half, my number came up, and they looked at the license and informed me, "Sir, you will have to take a driver's written test and a driving test—your license is expired two years and nine months!" Sigh. "Where do I go for that? Oh, to the Jefferson License Office? Where is that?" Sigh, sigh. Then I finally found it, next door to the Funeral Home where I had officiated many times.

When I got there, another crowd already waiting, I had to sit with a little slip of paper in my hand, waiting for another number. Finally, when my number came up, I approached (wearing Roman collar and warm coat!) the gentleman who looked at the license and informed me that I would have to take a driver's test on one of the computers there at hand. No problem.

My thoughts were not nice—"I know how to drive—I've been driving 65 years and I know all the rules—I've had only one parking ticket in my life, and will have a breeze doing this junk. I've even driven trucks, etc., etc." Sigh. Then, I hurried up, took it, and flunked the darned test!

"What do I do now, Sir?" His answer—"Go home, look up and study those driving rules on the Internet, and come back tomorrow at 8:00 am, to take it again. Besides, since you were expired for over two years, you will also have to take a road test" Oh, sigh, sigh, sigh.

So, I spent the afternoon studying the rules: blah, blah, blah. The next morning, I got there early to get to the head of the line and found that I was number 26 behind all those other early people who all had the same idea. So, once again, hurry and wait. The line moved quickly when it began and, once again, I found myself at the same computer, facing all those questions, now with much more attention, and concentration. And I passed it!

Heading for my place amid the crowd, I waited for a young slip of a girl to head my way, with a paper. She called my name, and we headed to my car, now very carefully so as not to again make some dumb mistake. If she had asked for us to travel to Australia, I would not have been surprised and would have immediately set out to do that, at her command. But no.

"Good morning, Miss. I'm Father Roy." Silence. "Turn right at the next corner." "Miss, do you do many of these tests?" "Some." Silence. "Turn left at the next corner." So, I realize that I'm not going to make friends and influence people in this endeavor, and just drive and shut up. Finally, the most beautiful words of the day: "Stop at the right of the door, and take this paper. Good day." And gone. My reaction—mumble, mumble, mumble, but now more humble and much less sure of myself. I think Miss Personality was even gladder than I was to be finished.

And you can be assured that now, every time I bring out my license, I will look at it and scrutinize the dates of the expiration, and thank God that I am now legal. Plus, I know that if I am driving 55 mph, I will be able to stop not within 372 feet, but within 350 feet. Dear Lord, have mercy!

## STORY 60: A TREASURE FOR ME AND FOR MANY:

How the People Program came to us.

It was the year 2003, and Gene Barnes had an idea. He and Tiny, his wife, had attended a program sponsored by the Sisters of St. Joseph on Mirabeau Avenue and found that it might solve our problem of a ministry geared to the "above 50 year olds" in our parish. So, one day, he, Deacon Tom Guntherberg, and I arranged to go there and observe. (In my mind, I really thought that it might be just a "Bingo Thing" for the elderly, but I was enlightened that day).

The director Mary Catherine Lombard gave us a tour of the facility (at the site of the former Novitiate for the Sisters, with a large yard, much parking, and all on one floor: no need for an elevator). The Program was renting the buildings from the Sisters. As we toured the place and observed some of the classes, it became more and more interesting and appealing to all of us. It might really do the trick and also appeal not only to our Holy Spirit People but to all of the West Bank, including the down-river and West Jefferson parishes, none of whom had anything of that sort.

And when we made the offer to the Sisters, rent-free, we urged that we be a satellite of their program (begun some 30 years before) in conjunction with them. They called it "Life-time Learning" and, at the time, had about 600 people attending many sorts of classes in dance, computers, needle work, language, music, ceramics, etc., lasting two semesters in the year: 15 classes for a minimal amount of tuition, all taught by volunteers. It seemed like what we were looking for. Little did we know it would grow into a great ministry, for that is what it was and still is.

And so we began the People Program West Bank Campus, with nearly 200 people registered and in place, with Mary Catherine and Delores Heglar directing: more than 50 teachers, composed of people who gave of their time and interest and skill. But God had plans.

After a year and a half of classes here, progressively improving, the People Program West Bank was in place, with much socializing, friendship, and learning skills growing each semester. Then August 29, 2005, Hurricane Katrina moved in, altering the lives of people and People. The campus at Mirabeau took on a flood of seven feet, destroying the files, materials, the hopes of the Sisters, and their buildings. And to make matters even worse, in the aftermath of the flood, their buildings caught fire and were destroyed: the end of an era.

So began a crusade looking for other location(s) for the East Bank. Being on the Board of Directors, Gene Barnes and I traveled all over New Orleans, now recovering from a flood which had covered over 80% of the city. We visited and inquired of many churches as to the possibility of their hosting the Program, at last count 19 of them, and were found wanting.

Finally, Mary Catherine and her helpers got a strike—from the large Methodist Church on Jeff Davis Parkway and Canal Street. They had been hosting large numbers of volunteers in town to help people dig their way out of the results of the flood and could give us space, at least for a couple of years. And so began another location on the East Bank.

The Methodist Pastor at this church called Mary Catherine, and we were given a location in Metairie—St. Michael Methodist Church, in West Metairie, a lovely location—all on one floor, with much off street parking. Another campus, now still going strong.

Since those chaotic days following the storms, the West Bank People Program has become increasingly interesting, satisfying, and fun. Mary Catherine and her husband, Michel, returned to his native France to live, and Delores Hegler took over, doing a fantastic job of continuing the Program, with the help of Doris Manuel and the volunteer teachers. It gets progressively better, as more and different classes are offered, among them, painting, art, story, and music.

A footnote. When we began our classes here, as an attempt at humor, I volunteered to teach a class I called "Cajun Culture." And surprisingly, it became a hit—we had large enrollments for nine semesters: Cajun music, cuisine, dance, religious practices, and color. Someone once asked me, "What do you mean, 'Cajun culture??' Sounds like a conundrum contradiction—Cajun and culture?" My response to that was, "Don't forget that feeling when you hear a good Cajun joke, do a Zydeco dance, or face a good dish of crawfish etouffee, you hear?"

Now, in another direction, we began a very popular class called "Listening to Good Music" led by Caryl "Tiny" Barnes, a great teacher and piano player. It's been going for four semesters, with another semester facing us, after our listening to great American Music.

In the meantime, on the Lake Front, the Sisters purchased the former Lutheran Student Union in the UNO area to become the main campus. A new overall Director, Laverne Kappel, was selected and put in place, with Jan Martino assisting her, with offices at the Lakefront location. And we are fortunate that Delores continues here to do such a great job of keeping everything going, with many people (upwards of 200) registered for the fall session.

This has been a good program, and continues to be so: a treasure I look back upon with much satisfaction.

## STORY 61: WHAT IT WAS LIKE TO ENTER THE SEMINARY

It was August 26, 1946; World War II was over, and I had graduated from St. Joseph Academy the June before, after the 11<sup>th</sup> grade. An exciting time—we had gotten through the Great Depression, then recovery, as the war ground to a stop and then life went on.

The Christmas before, I began to realize that, at the end of that school year, life for me would change very drastically. Being the oldest of three boys, I had an important place in Daddy's shop. Daddy had long spoken about my entering LSU and studying accounting to become an auditor, which did not appeal to me, but he needed me, and so I agreed to do so. We all worked in the shop with him.

As I reflected on my life, I realized that I had been blessed with a happy home, good parents, and a rich life. In grammar school, I had had a friend named Jimmy Lacour who entered the seminary at St. Ben's, and after four years was to graduate at the same time as I did. But he wrote to me that, although he liked the seminary, he wanted a family, so after graduation, he would leave and return home. I listened to his stories, and, as I did so, I became more and more attracted to that sort of life even though I knew very little about any of it, and I had never really been away from home.

Another factor in my life was that my mother's parain was a priest of long standing in the diocese of Alexandria. Once he visited us in New Roads, and I was impressed. He was smart, up to date, and spoke well about his life. Besides, he was an American and a Cajun. (As it happened, he preached at my first Mass, and a year later, he was dead of prostate cancer.)

Up until then, I had never met any other priest but the many Dutch pastors. Fr. John Hoes was my first occasion of knowing a priest—he was a holy man and gentle. When he died in 1942, he was replaced by another Dutch priest, Fr. John Janssens, who was not as warm as Fr. Hoes. In fact, his way was more distant and. at times, cold and strict.

One of his favorite expressions to me was, "Roy, you talk too much! Shut up." And I can honestly say, I never heard from him any word of encouragement about anything. Rather, it was, "Listen. Mister, you don't know a thing. Get out of the way and let me do this right!" He was a good enough pastor, but no warmth until after I was ordained, and then it was only acceptance, almost begrudgingly.

During the time between Fr. Hoes and Fr. Janssens, for about six months, Fr. Charles Plauche (a distant cousin—Mom had been a Plauche) came and was our temporary pastor at St. Mary's. And it was like the sun coming out—an interesting man, well educated, also a Cajun, and an attractive life opened up for me. And I think that did it for me. After he left, this began to be my direction.

During my time in school, I discussed the priesthood with the Sisters and with my parents, especially with my mother, and with Steve Patin, a young man from our neighborhood who was to graduate at St. Ben's from junior college. He started helping me with my Latin, even while he revealed to me that he would not return to the seminary when his class entered Notre Dame Seminary in New Orleans in the fall. He was a help to me—Latin was a challenge.

Steve gave me some of his books and helped me to mentally prepare to take the steps I would take. Mom and I had to insist with Fr. Janssens that he apply for me to enter at the end of that summer, with Allen Langlois who would enter in first year of high school.

Allen and I were given an appointment to meet with Archbishop Rummel at Notre Dame Seminary to discuss the seminary and apply for entrance. But Fr. J wasn't inclined to go with us, so Lucy stepped in. She told him, "Father, if you don't go with us, then let's forget the whole thing—and I'll let Fr. Plauche (who was now Chancellor of the Archdiocese of New Orleans) know how you feel about all this." That did the trick—he asked me to drive us all in his car. We were accepted and started making plans and getting all that we needed to be ready.

The Langlois family and mine came to St. Ben's in August: I had my heart in my mouth. They were going to leave me there, even if I wanted to be there. St. Ben's was and is a beautiful place—a large campus, with about 400 young men in high school and junior college, from all over Louisiana, especially the Lafayette diocese and the Archdiocese.

When my folks left, it was a difficult time, but that quickly passed—new people, new subjects in class, new challenges (not at all as it was with my family, who had never been without me!) I quickly took to the lifestyle. The monks were and continue to be great friends of mine: St. Ben's is like another home for me.

During the war years, the school had been 11 months of the year (the draft, you know), and the college seminarians would jump a year in their formation, while the high schoolers would not. When this "empty year" reached college level, the faculty chose twelve from the senior class to study during the summer, to graduate a couple of years ahead of time. Fortunately, I was in that group, with two classmates, Les Prescott and Gene Lafleur, both of Opelousas. This was a challenge, but we were ready, and rejoiced on this happening.

Two years of Philosophy and four of Theology, and, in 1954, we were ordained to the Priesthood. As to my going to LSU to study accounting and auditing, Daddy told me, "If this is really what you feel you want, then go ahead, but whatever you do, make sure that you give it your all. And you have our blessing." The rest is history.

## STORY 62: JESUS, BORN A GIRL?

The Angel Gabriel returned from his trip to earth where he began the process of our Redemption—announcing to Mary that she would be a mother, not just any ordinary motherhood, you understand. "You will bear a son, and you are to name him 'Jesus' because he will save his people from their sins," he tells her. And from that remarkable conversation, we can use our imagination to reflect upon all that that implies.

WHAT IF . . . ?

— Mary had refused? Read Luke's Gospel.
— he had said, "You will bear a daughter?" Now that would have really changed it all.
— he had spoken to Joseph instead and offered him that same arrangement?
— she already had children? Unlikely, but possible.
— Joseph had previously had children of his own? Some say he did have.

Those "curves" bring changes (or challenges?) into all the infancy narratives of Luke and Matthew, don't they? How we have so imbibed unquestionably the story of Jesus as a man and not as a woman. But when we consider that eventuality, it opens up a world that we're not used to considering, and sometimes, for some, it's not a comfortable consideration!

But it's a fruitful possibility—and we are to use our imagination when we're dealing with Sacred Scripture, and where it leads us. The Scriptures are so rich in bringing us inspiration, devotion, even an expansion of our appreciation of the "Good News" and how it provides us with a path to our

God and God's goodness to us. It affects us in our prayer, our ministry, our self-concept, and our community. This all has to do with our health.

I once brought up the possibility of what it would have meant had Jesus been born a woman. And the reaction I received was that I was offering a consideration which was mystifying, unholy, even blasphemous, eliciting a response much as one of my graduate school professors received when he sang (in jest, of course) "Surprise! there is no God, and we have fooled all the people!" We laughed it off, but it was an unexpected suggestion. And in the '60's, it was not an unusual occurrence as we went through the iconoclasm of the time, some arising from Vatican II, some good, and some not so comfortable.

To have lived through that time (Vatican II was from 1962-65) was to uncover much overturning of some of our old ghosts and their mindsets: liturgical, canonical, pious, and devotional. And the opposition to the "more modern thinking" is still around us.

So many people feel that they have to defend God—if you don't think that's a fact, I suggest that you say you think Jesus should have been born a woman (after you make sure that you're wearing a helmet and a bulletproof vest!). Plus, many people think that they have to defend the Church or the "holy" against any kind of thinking that they feel is heretical, schismatic, agnostic, or atheistic. And all the while, we are urged to use our imagination: to let us be free to wonder and find the awe in God's dealings with us.

## STORY 63: Having your ideas trampled on

This story begins in the summer of 1966. I was assigned by a call from Archbp. Hannan asking me to take the parish of St. Joseph in Chauvin as Pastor, with an Assistant Pastor. I had been ordained 14 years, and was 39 years old. This parish had two missions—one at Cocodrie, 15 miles away, and the other, 8 miles away, at Upper Little Caillou: about 2,000 families: Cajun.

The fear I had in accepting this request was the school. Four hundred students, middle and senior high level, with twenty teachers; an almost completed new church and its debt. This was a challenge, besides which I was being asked to replace a great priest whose shoes would be difficult to follow in. He could do everything well. But, because I was being asked by the Archbishop to take this parish, I could not refuse: my predecessor was being asked to be Rector of a new idea: a High School Seminary. So, with all enthusiasm, I accepted it and obeyed, but with much trepidation: I had never had to contend before with a Catholic school as Administrator.

I had little idea how to proceed. The area had had sparse educational opportunity, besides having a great deal of poverty, so tuition would be a problem. Prior to that time, the Archdiocese had been subsidizing the school, and now I was informed I would have to make up the deficits without such help. Very quickly, I made many friends who would support me who today remain as close to me as my family. We agreed to set up a school board, and Home and School association. School athletics and coaches were uppermost in all minds.

All but two members of our faculty had to travel at least 15 miles to get to the school. There were many expectations among them. Daily, I and my associate were in the school teaching religion classes, but the array of running a church parish with all its demands ran right on. We had a very full schedule. By the time I had been there six months, I came up with a full-blown case of Shingles!

By the end of the first year, I realized that there existed a spirit among the coaches that I was the wrong man in the wrong place. I detected reluctance and subtle apathy in spite of all I did to achieve a unified spirit. Sports, and especially football, were uppermost in the minds of our teachers, the families whose students we were trying to bring out of darkness, and especially our coaches, all six of them.

And then one night, three years after I entered that scene, our church rectory burned down in January, 1969. All our belongings, books, clothes, and "stuff" were destroyed. But we pushed on. People helped us out with a collection and sympathy, as we moved into another parish, five miles away. A new rectory was planned, along with a visitation by the Southern Association of Colleges and Schools for accreditation and excellence. By October, we were accepted, and, along the way, I quit smoking, cold turkey.

One major mistake I made was to appoint, (with the agreement of the School Board) the head football coach as principal, replacing an excellent Benedictine Sister who remained with us to teach. Moving the school from Religious Sisters to the laity seemed to be the best direction to take, at the time. But gradually, I detected a void growing between the school and the church parish, not only with the teachers, but also in the minds of the parents of our students, and so, too, with our students. The coaches were the determining decision-makers, as the budgets began to be trampled, without care of how to cover the expenses. It was not a happy time for me: I was so alone in many situations.

By the time I was there for five years, I began to wonder at the wisdom of my and our situation. My spiritual director advised me that, since it was such a stressful assignment, we would have to cancel the 1971 school year: the financial plight we were in had no ready solution. We had begun, in 1968, a fund-raiser for the school which we called "Lagniappe on the Bayou," to feature Cajun foods, crafts, music, games, and focus onto our Cajun background. It was a huge success, even if, as our publicity grew, the spotlight came to rest on us. We had hard liquor and serious gambling as part of the Fair.

A later Bishop ruled that it was unseemly for the Church to have to depend on such activities for its stewardship demands, and rightly so. The prohibition of such elements came through after I was re-assigned to begin a new parish in Algiers.

I left there with a heavy heart, feeling that all my efforts had been subverted, and we had failed. But the real test about the wisdom of closing the school has been that the school buildings today, almost 40 years later, are still empty, except for catechism classes and the occasional marine and Coast Guard workshops on safety. And yet, I wonder if someone else could have done better, and avoided the pain which, mercifully, has subsided. I am honored to have lived so much of that history, and more than survived it all, so long ago.

## STORY 64: "A Wise Person—Seven years detached—Why Wise?"

There are seldom people I meet whom I find are not wise. Smart? Yes. Clever? Yes. But wise is something which is much deeper. To be wise (for me) is someone whose life, personality, interests, attention, and "smarts" make me look up to them in their dealings with other people. Wise is rather indefinable. They may be outgoing and gregarious; they may be introspective and have to be coaxed out to express their own thoughts. But wisdom is a God-given quality, as we see when we read the Book of Wisdom.

"Therefore I prayed, and prudence was given me. I pleaded, and the spirit of Wisdom came to me. I preferred her to scepter and throne . . . Yet all good things together came to me in her company, and countless riches at her hands: I rejoiced in them all because Wisdom is their leader, though I had not known that she is the mother of these." (Wisdom 7:7 ff).

The wise person I want to suggest is my mother. There are instances when I wished she had not expressed her feelings so quickly and openly; also, when she made up her mind, she was already into implementing the suggestion and its direction. But, back of all that, there was a faith, a warmth, a reality of strong hope, and an embracing of "the other" which manifested her wisdom. There was a real goodness and openness to the Will of God and to what she saw as God's demands, which were to be obeyed and entertained by all means. I don't think that I ever saw Mom in any argument.

She was great at suggesting, coaxing, and urging, but never confronting. I don't think that I ever heard her belittle anyone. Rather, when she saw someone in a "tight spot," her inclination was to reach out and comfort that person in need—"Pauve cher, c'est triste; allons voire si il n'ya pas quelque chose, ons peut faire pour eux-autres." ("Let's help them, pauvre bête.")

Some of the prized moments when I tasted her wisdom (Mom died in August, 2001), were times when I would drive home and Mom would be waiting with a fresh pot of coffee and hours to share her and my triumphs with me but also to extend to me the comfort which I sometimes badly needed. She had tasted much grief with family illnesses (of her ten siblings, four of them were dead by twenty-five years of age). From a farming family, she knew hard work, and sometimes taking a risk to survive—they were flooded out in the "high water of 1927."

Her deep faith served her well—Daddy always said that he learned his Faith from her and her family. Her spirit of fun also endeared her to all of us: she loved to sing (she told me that, in connection with her morning devotion, she would pick out a hymn "which went around my head all day long").

When I was in the Army at Ft. Sill, Oklahoma, she came to visit for a week. After she returned home, Daddy informed me that, "You'll never do that again—I missed her too much!"

My favorite scripture passage is, "As a mother comforts her son, so will I comfort you, says the Lord." And she lived this out in her life.

## STORY 65: Words, La Parole: How we take some of God's gifts so much for granted!

The gift of word is one of them. We learn words as a child, growing our vocabulary, from "Momma" (the Latin word for the breast "to be fed") to much longer and more meaningful words, coming to us from our roots. Greek? Babylonian? Cajun? Funny, but I never noticed that the French language has no "th" sound. Where do you think "Who dat?" comes from? Like "Antony from the nint' wahd." I learned something. Rounding our "dese and dose" marks us to others.

The sound is how we Cajuns count: one, two, tree! Or tirteen. What do we do about our vowels? "a, e, i, o, u, y"—all a vowel is is a speaking sound produced when we don't allow any sound to interfere with the sound coming from the voice. The most prominent sound in a syllable. And we hear that the ancient Hebrew language had no consonants! Dat do make t'ings tough.

And yet, John's Gospel begins with, "In the beginning was the Word, and the Word was God . . . The Word was made flesh and dwelt among us." A Word spoken by the mouth of God—Jesus Christ. Even those words handed down to us from Scripture have been such an influence to us and our way of life—words like potato chips—"the more you eat, the more you want." Without words, how destitute we are. And to be able to read is quite a gift—we are blessed to be able to read.

When we consider it, words not only deal life, but they also deal death. Consider what Hitler did with words: 20 million people died because of his use of words, especially "We are the master race!" He brought to his people the way out of bankruptcy but couldn't stop there, and he led those people into so much death. All because of a word.

Words also deal life. Reflect on the marriage covenant, done with a word: "I, John, take you, Mary, to be my wife . . . I will love you and honor you all the days of my life!" And how those words touch our lives and our loves in the life they engender. Other words also, "This is my Body; this is my Blood. Take this and eat . . . drink: Do this in remembrance of me!" These words also bring about life at a much deeper level. They enable us to offer once again in an unbloody manner, the Body and Blood of Jesus, . . . "All glory and honor, forever and ever!" Amen.

In a moral aside, it behooves us to remain careful how we use our ability to make word. In French, "La Parole" is our word—it is used in the legal community as someone once incarcerated is released "on his word: paroled!" He is given his liberty to remain at large as long as he does not violate his word. Also, when a Cajun tells you, "Il m'a pas addresse la parole" (He didn't speak a word to me), we see how lack of communication and its necessity can affect and hurt people because they were ignored. And, when someone tells me, "I give you my word," I know that I can rightly have confidence in that person because his word is his bond and worth trusting.

## STORY 66: "A Great and Needed Kindness"

It was September 9th, 1965, and Hurricane Betsy had roared through St. Bernard Parish the night before. As Pastor of Our Lady of Lourdes Church in Violet, I and my Associate Fr. Benny had endured the night in the Rectory without even a thought of evacuating. The wind had switched at about 10:30 and we knew that the worst, the "eye," had passed. There was no power and not any of the present benefits of communication which we have today, so we were unaware of what wreckage had been wreaked upon our people and our four churches "down below."

To find out, the three Eucharistic Missionary Sisters came with us in my car. We drove about only 8 miles until we got to the Civil Defense Shelter at St. Bernard High School and found not only water and wreckage everywhere, but about a thousand people marooned from our missions further down the road. They were without leadership. The shelter director had tried the evening before to move them to Chalmette. When they refused, he left and went home, leaving all those families stranded without water, radio communication, or food. What to do—it was 5:30 in the morning?

Looking over the situation, I consulted with some of our parishioners in the shelter and decided to pitch in to relieve the fears, the stresses, and the exposure of our people. I had been assigned to that area several years before, so I already knew and loved them.

First, I walked down the street to Mrs. Leona's, the cafeteria director at the school, and found that she, with her school cafeteria staff, had a store room with all her commodities intact, and she could feed large numbers of people. She agreed to open up the cafeteria and begin organizing all those people into some sort of way to bring aid for the adults and children staying there. I drove to the hardware store up the road and bought three large plastic garbage cans with covers to carry clean water into the cafeteria.

I learned to siphon—it enabled me to get water from a large cistern (and also to get gasoline, later on). We made coffee and were relieved when the aroma of that coffee began to bring some sort of normalcy to all those frightened huddled people scattered in the gymnasium, the school office, and the schoolrooms. No phone, no radio, none of the Civil Defense people around—it was up to us—sink or swim.

People began to come up to ask me questions, and I realized that I had to take charge if we were to make it through. So we formed a team which would take care of spaces and duties for the families, food preparation, and bathroom order, besides having some sort of police authority so that the inhabitants of the shelter would be able to last through until we could have some sort of contact with the outside world. After all, we were stranded there.

This lasted about two weeks; the stress level daily was very high. When the usual context of families has evaporated, fears are elevated, anger is close by, and survival is threatened.

Somehow we reached a level of acceptance and order until outside help reached us, which eventually it did, with the arrival of soldiers and trucks from the National Guard and their loads of bottled water, cots, and blankets which all promised that leadership would also come in a take charge. Many of our people had found ways to get down to their homes in Delacroix Island, Reggio, Yscloskey, and Hopedale where the wreckage was fierce.

One incident: someone reported to me that the men's large school bathrooms were clogged up (and still no running water!) When I went to investigate, it was baadddd! Then I recalled that the fire station up the road still had their fire truck! I knew the local firemen, and, when the truck came to the shelter, I myself took the firehose and, with them, began to flush those toilets. Nasty, nasty, nasty but needed. And while this was occurring, someone came to tell me that Bishop Caillouet, my former pastor, had arrived and wanted to see me.

Obviously, people would be able to drive through from outside St. Bernard Parish, so help was on the way. So, when the Bishop came to see me and my messy self, I asked if, when I could get out of the shelter, he would see me. This occurred two days later, after I was be able to clean myself up to be presentable.

The night that I got out of the shelter, I drove to Holy Rosary rectory early in the evening. Bishop Caillouet, during the three years while I had been his assistant there, had been a good friend to me: he was a good pastor (he, ten years before, had ordained our class because Archbishop Rummel was no longer able to see enough to ordain us.) So, his coming there after the stress of the Storm and its aftermath was such a great kindness he extended to me.

For a couple of hours, I poured out all my fears, my hesitations, and my angers, but also the human foibles which I had experienced during that terrible time. And he listened. A couple of times, I saw his eyes flutter, but he stayed there without flinching. Then, I asked if I could receive the sacrament of reconciliation, which he gladly offered me. Peace. I had used language that belonged to the National Guard and not to a priest, but at the time I felt it had to be done, and the Bishop never interrupted me.

Now, forty years later, I still am grateful. Not only for his kindness, but also for his great priestliness. Bishop Abel Caillouet has been dead for almost 20 years, and I still recall on the anniversary of his death, his gentle friendship. A great priestly gift.

## STORY 67: Thoughts on a theme by John Donne: "No Man Is an Island": (1572-1631).

Maybe he for whom this bell tolls may be so sick that he knows not that it tolls for him, and maybe I may think myself so much better than I am, as they who are about me, and see my state, may have caused it to toll for me, and I am unaware of that. The Church is catholic and universal; so are all her actions; all that she does belongs to all.

When she (the Church) baptizes a child, that action concerns me; for that child is thereby connected to that body which is my head, too, and ingrafted into that body of which I am a member.

When she buries a man, that action concerns me: all mankind is of one Author and is one volume; when one man dies, one chapter is not torn out of the book but translated into a better language; and every chapter must be so translated; God employs several translators; some pieces are translated by age, some by sickness, some by war, some by justice; but God's hand is in every translation, and his hand shall bind up all our scattered pages again for that library where every book shall lie open to one another.

If we understand aright the dignity of this bell that tolls for our evening prayer, we would be glad to make it ours by rising early, in this way that it might be ours as well as his whose indeed it is. The bell doth toll for him that think it does, and though it rings again, yet from that minute that that occasion is brought upon him, he is united to God. Who casts not up his eye to the sun when it rises? But who takes off his eye from a comet when that breaks out? Who bends not his ear to any bell which upon any occasion rings? But who can remove it from that bell which is passing a piece of himself out of this world?

"NO MAN IS AN ISLAND, entire of itself; every man is a piece of the Continent, a part of the main. If a clod of dirt is washed away by the sea, Europe is the less, as well as if a promontory were, as well as if a manor of your friend's or of your own were (washed away); any man's death diminishes me, because I am involved in mankind; and, therefore, never send to know FOR WHOM THE BELL TOLLS; it tolls for thee (Donne).

Neither can we call this a begging of misery or a borrowing of misery, as though we were not miserable enough of ourselves, but must fetch in more from the next house, in taking upon ourselves the misery of our neighbors. Our God is our only security.

## STORY 68: A SIBLING, Me and Jerry:

My story is about my brother Jerry and me when we lived on St. Jude Street. It was about 1939: I was 12 and Jerry 9. Mom called me in and gave me five pennies and told me to take Jerry with me and walk the three blocks to buy a nickel box of wooden matches at "Miss Clo's" store. Both of us had been to Miss Clo's and knew that she was a difficult person who was not at all congenial. In fact, "Elle est mauvaise: une veuve qui amie pas des enfants" (She's a mean widow and doesn't like kids). Plus, she was what in these days, we would call obese: 50 years old and had no husband or children, but did have arthritis.

Miss Clo's store was not really a store—it was what today we would call a storefront. On the corner of Morningside and Main Streets, she had a glass front building with glass counters where she had bread, candy, milk, eggs, but little else. You didn't go shopping in those days, and you certainly wouldn't shop at Miss Clo's.

So, Jerry and I, barefooted, walked to get the wooden matches. (At home, we had a fireplace for which we cut kindlings and sawed tree logs to keep warm in the winter, also wood for the cast iron stove in the kitchen, for cooking). Five pennies in those days was an "amount."

When we got to Miss Clo's, we entered the store and went to the counter. Her greeting was: "What do you want, boy?" I reached into my pocket and brought out the "amount"—four pennies. "Momma wants a box of matches." Her response: "You got only four pennies, boy—you need five: where's the other penny?" "I don't know; I must have lost it on the way here."

"Well, you little scamp, don't think that I'm going to give you anything. I think that you're trying to steal from me, and I don't like it! I'm not giving you nothing—so you and your little brother get back home and tell your Momma to punish you for not only trying to take my money, but you tried to lie to me! Not get on home; pense donc, le 'tit' monstre voler mon argent!" And away we went. Nice lady. The whole question went from matches to pennies!

When I got back home, Mom heard the story and, instead of her fussing about it, she just accepted it all and didn't insist. Miss Clo acquired another person who couldn't stand her and would never send us to buy something there again. No accusations, because she trusted Jerry and me—we had lost that penny somehow and were not lying. I still don't know where that lost penny went. "Jamais de la vie!"

It's strange how today a penny is not worth picking up from the ground, but, in those days, it was the context for someone being mean and cross and tight. And so it was in a small town on the banks of False River in Depression time.

## STORY 69: "A Gift Lost Before I Really Received It"

It as Christmas of 1940; we were living on St. Jude Street (which is probably for me where I was really home!). I was 11 years old; my two brothers were (Jerry and Kearn younger than I). I was in the 7th grade in school, the year I entered high school, and I was a happy Cajun.

We were coming out of the Depression, and money was becoming meaningful and available for us—we picked pecans; I delivered groceries at Deville's Grocery and so enjoyed the band and its music. We looked forward to the Santa Claus event with our family in Hamburg where all our cousins would gather for Mass and then the distribution of gifts in our grandparents' home.

When Santa came in, everyone was present. All the "Ho-ho-hoes" took place as my grandma kept calling Santa a "she" (the French for Santa was "La Sainte Christine"—which is feminine, so she wasn't wrong). The gifts began floating, and, suddenly, Jerry and I had these long packages—looking good.

Jerry opened his first, and I saw with great joy that Santa had given us each a bow and arrow set. (Of course, I also saw that the arrows had rubber tips, so it wasn't a "real bow and arrow set"). Anyway, I liked what I saw. Jerry took his bow out and held it up. I got mine and opened it up. It was a beauty. I had wanted one of those for a long time. I ripped off the paper and held the bow at arms length. When I strung the bow string to the two ends, it was all I could do not to pull on the string to try to see if I was strong enough to pull it. And when I held the bow in my left hand, I pulled with my right, and the bow suddenly, with a loud crack, broke right above where I was holding it in my left hand. I was heart-broken.

Of course, Daddy saw what had happened and assured me that he "could fix it by making a splice and it would be as strong as a new one." But the beauty lost its beauty—it was broken and would never be the same. Gloom and a spoiled Christmas.

Later on, Daddy did fix it, but it was clumsy, and I was "Coeur-casse"—"Creve-coeur". We returned to New Roads. Jerry, of course, loved his bow and arrow, and I had to watch the beauty of it, while mine had that splint. Even when you're poor, you can be spoiled, and I was.

We shot our arrows and learned to do quite well. But, with high school beginning for me, other attentions interfered, and life went on. When March came around, we made kites and flew them (even if our kites seemed always to be drawn to the limbs of tall trees).

Sure enough, one day as my kite was flying high, it began to make those crazy circles that kites make and landed in the tall pecan tree on Mr. Paul Hebert's lot next door. I pulled on the string, and this only made it worse, so I decided I would try to get it loose with one of my arrows. I tied a long needle to the end of the arrow, and, when I shot it at my kite, the arrow stuck in the large limb near the kite and lodged there. No kite and no arrow. That was the end of my archery experience.

## STORY 70: A Day Never to be Forgotten

Being ordained a priest is a very memorable event—you prepare for it in so many ways over many years, and the ordination itself is beyond words. Every year you and your classmates observe it with alumni occasions. As time goes on and you age, you begin to look forward to anniversaries of significance. Somehow it seems that you were born a priest.

In our time, we had the junior clergy and its annual exams to endure. Older (and supposedly more knowledgeable) priests would meet with our group of "five-year-ordained" priests to be questioned about theology, history, canon law, and liturgy. It brought us back to the seminary, where we went through those tests; but, once we were ordained six years, it was over.

The next big event was our tenth anniversary. We looked upon those "young whippersnappers" who followed us as we increasingly included them in our social (and church) life and became more solid friends. Annual occasions provided socialization with them, such as parish confirmations, forty-hour devotions, vacations spent together, stations of the cross, and alumni meetings. Many of them were assigned to our home parishes, and we used the occasion to note their approach to the ministry of people and what we could learn from them to improve our own preaching, hearing of confessions, and liturgies—especially preparing for funerals and dealing with death among our parishioners.

A great step occurred when we came to our Silver Anniversary. We prepared for it with our people, and, when it arrived, we already began to feel the approach of death—especially when one of our ordination classes had departed. It can be a sobering time. And, of course, the onset of aging manifested itself and touched us. Perhaps illness is part of that journey; it clarifies the reality that life is not some sort of playground but is serious business. We had been so healthy that we began to believe that life owed us many, many years. Then we were brought back to concerns about health, balance in our lives—along with prayer, continuing education, and an outlook on the future. We looked at the "senior clergy" and perhaps wondered if we were going to one day ever be in that number.

And then the day of our Golden Jubilee approached. We didn't really think we would ever be part of that group (or did we really believe that we would live forever?). But it arrived, as we woke up deeply grateful. (In the past, those were the old fogies who were "on the October side of the Hill," and now we are among them. Can it be?) The numbers in our class have declined (now there are more, seemingly, of our friends on the other side of the grave than are on this side!). We have so many to thank for where we are—friends, classmates, teachers, and loving people who have given and now give our lives value and joy. And when that day of our Golden Jubilee has passed, it takes on even more meaning with the humility that tells us that so much of life is GIFT, and we pray that we will continue to savor it, all in God's time and God's hands.

It has been a good life, and I am deeply grateful for the gift which comes to me everyday, from the first wonderful cup of coffee to "Now I lay me down to sleep; I pray the Lord, my soul to keep . . . Amen, thank you, O, Lord!"

# STORY 71: ". . . What Was I Thinking . . . !?"

When, in 1972, I was offered to begin a new parish, I began with stars in my eyes—no doubts, no fears, all excitement: raring to go. I had been a priest for 18 years and a pastor for eight. Having been pastor in Chauvin for six of those years, with all of its fears and uncertainties, I was looking forward to getting involved with another community (even with its "unchartedness"), a community of a different kind, in another area, from rural, country, Cajun, to a suburb of New Orleans, with the pastoral enthusiasm coming out of the Second Vatican Council.

That we had no name for this new endeavor, no land on which to build, and no money in the bank, and last but not least, we were being carved out from another thriving parish whose pastor had petitioned for another parish, but who had changed his mind when it didn't go his way—all this I now look back on and ask myself, "What was I thinking?"—and further, "Was I thinking at all???" I now wonder that, if I had to do it all again, would I have skipped into that situation with less enthusiasm than I did?

I realized the challenge facing us. I felt the sting of so many "contrarians" whose words about us were, "They don't do things like we do!" Or, "Well, that won't last!" Or, (and this did happen), "Roy, when are you going to get to work in a real parish and stop fooling around: you don't even have your own church?" "You and your parish are parasites!" Sigh. "When are you going to get out of that Protestant church and get into a real church?"

Having to move out of Our Lady of Holy Cross Chapel and into the Mary Joseph Residence for the Elderly was a shaking shock. But we thrived there—loved the elderly who welcomed our people, especially the children, into their midst. But 18 months later when their ground floor began to subside, the shock came home. Fear. Uncertainty. What to do? Where will we go?

We were able to welcome the large Vietnamese contingent into our midst, but now, what?

Meeting and discussing with the parish folks was a memorable event. We met in one of their day rooms (with its billiards table in the rear), our people standing around or sitting on the floor. Questions such as, "Father, where will we go; why continue to struggle; there are eight churches in our area—why another one?" "We haven't really begun our parish life: why not just close it down before we make more mistakes?" "What was I thinking?"

And then came in the mail the invitations from two of our fellow churches who had worked with us helping the Vietnamese get settled into our area. St. Stephen Lutheran, and St. Philip Episcopal Church, and their overwhelming Christian spirit—"Father, you have no place, and we have—these spaces not ours but are only here in trust. Come, share them with us—space, schedule, rent, calendars can be worked out. Join with us, and we'll make out!" I was and still am so touched by their generosity and openness to the will of a good God. Our choice of St. Philip's began an odyssey which has so enriched my own life and that of so many people. And, as Moses, who experienced at the River Jordan before his people entered the land of milk and honey, said, "Remember where you came from and how you got to where you now are—it is due to a good God and his love for you. Never forget that—it is all gift!" And so it is today: we are grateful.

## STORY 72: LIFE AFTER BIRTH

**This is a story that I like to use as a sermon because of the message that it conveys. I don't know who the author of the story is, and I can't remember where I got the story**

**from, but it has become one of my favorites over the years. I hope that my readers will enjoy it as much as I do.**

Once upon a time, twin boys were conceived in the womb. Seconds, minutes, hours passed as the two tiny lives developed. The spark of life grew, and each tiny brain began to take shape and form. With the development of the brain came feeling, and, with feeling, perception—a perception of surroundings, of each other, and of their own lives. They discovered that life was good, and they laughed and rejoiced in their hearts.

One said to the other, "We are so lucky to have been conceived and to have this wonderful world." The other chimed in, "Yes, blessed be our mother who gave us life and each other." Each of the twins continued to grow, and soon their arms and fingers, legs and toes began to take shape. They stretched their bodies and turned in their little world. They explored it and found the life cord, which gave them life from their mother's blood. They were grateful for this new discovery and sang, "How great is the love of our mother—that she shares all that she has with us!"

Weeks passed into months, and, with the advent of each new month, they noticed a change in each other and in themselves. "We are changing," one said. "What can it mean?" "It means," said the other, "that we are drawing near to birth." An unsettling chill crept over the two. They were afraid of birth, for they knew that it meant leaving their wonderful world behind. Said the one, "Were it up to me, I would live here forever."

"But we must be born," said the other. "It has happened to all the others." Indeed, there was evidence inside the womb that the mother had carried life before theirs. "And I believe that there is life after birth, don't you?"

"How can there be life after birth?" cried the one. "Do we not shed our life cord and also the blood tissue when we are born? And have you ever talked to anyone that has been born? Has anyone ever reentered the womb after birth to describe what birth is like? NO!" As he spoke, he fell into despair, and he moaned, "If the purpose of conception and our growth inside the womb is to end in birth, then truly our life is senseless." He clutched his precious life cord to his breast and said, "And, if this is so and life is absurd, then there really can be no mother!" "But, if there is a mother," protested the other, "Who else gave us nourishment? Who else created this world for us?"

"We get our nourishment from this cord—and our whole world has always been here," said the one. "If there is a mother, where is she? Have you ever seen her? Does she ever talk to you? No! We invented the mother when we were young because it satisfied a need in us. It made us feel secure and happy." Thus, while the one raved and despaired, the other resigned himself to birth and placed his trust in the hands of his mother. Hours turned into days, and days into weeks. And soon it was time. They both knew their birth was at hand, and they both feared what they did not know. As the one was first to be conceived, so he was the first to be born, the other following.

They cried as they were born into the light. They coughed out fluid and gasped the dry air. And, when they were sure they had been born, they opened their eyes—seeing life after birth for the very first time. What they saw was the beautiful eyes of their mother, as they were cradled lovingly in her arms. They were home. We, too, are home—Christians, called so for the very first time at Antioch.

## STORY 73: A TOTAL SURPRISE

It was an afternoon in 1989, and I was working in the church office, busy about parish work. A knock came at the door (the secretary had already finished work and gone home), and I opened it to find Bogy Boogaerts there holding a large brown envelope in his hands and having a strange look on his face—a look which usually meant that he had gotten something on me, or he had found something else about "Coonasses" to laugh about. He was good at that.

My question was the usual, "What's the matter, Bogy?" And all I got back was a laugh and a real "razzmatazz." "Ha, ha, ha—I knew it would come! Ha, ha!" Then he spilled it—"I got your mail—it just came in, Your Monsignorness!" And he was practically jumping up and down in to the office. "Reverend Monsignorness, Yes, that's a good title!"

I didn't know whether to laugh or cry, or both, or neither. "What's this all about? What's that large envelope you're carrying? Oh, 'Rev. Monsignor Allen Roy'. What's that all about? This looks official! It IS OFFICIAL! O my Lord, how could this be? We haven't had Monsignors in years in our Archdiocese. Bogy, you're sure you haven't cooked this up just to get my goat?"

And his only answer was, "Your Monsignorness, I like that; your Monsignorness, Go ahead, Father Roy, open it up. This comes from the Chancery Office and the Archbishop." And I did so, with so much consternation and wonder. It was a letter (in Latin, of course), saying that I had been honored by the Pope, no less. Then it read:

"I have the great pleasure of informing you that the Holy Father has issued a decree under date of the enclosed document granting you the rank of Honorary Prelate. I heartily congratulate you upon the reception of this well deserved honor which recognizes the contribution you have made to the spiritual welfare of those under your pastoral care, etc. etc., etc."

Well, it was a surprise, even with my own misgivings. I had been involved in forming a new parish, without too much evident success, and with much stress, but with much satisfaction in my heart with the people and what we had brought about here at Holy Spirit. Now that we had built a church and rectory, I hoped that it would be easier, and it turned out that it was. We grew, with many more families, a further building campaign to erect the Parish Family Life center (which now stands today to enable us to have had the People Program going for the past eight years).

And it turned out that I was one of the nineteen priests to be invested with the "Monsignorship"; we go one further. It is an honor, but one which is no longer what it was years ago when being a Monsignor really meant something priests strove for and rejoiced over or sometimes pined for, if unsuccessful.

Today, I think it is a relic of the past hierarchy of the "pecking order" in the Church on the local scene, and I choose to look at it as a recognition of good pastoral service. And that's all I have to say about it.

## STORY 74: AN EVENT OR BOOK WHICH CHANGED MY LIFE AND OUTLOOK

It was 1962, and I was Catholic Chaplain in the 159th Evacuation Hospital National Guard Unit mobilized by President John F. Kennedy to be a part of the situation with the Berlin Wall in Europe. Without any warning, we were called to operate the Mash Hospital at Fort Sill, Oklahoma, all without any hint of what the future would hold for us. All we knew was that we were in the Army, to report on August 26th. I had been chaplain for about five years when this happened.

Our Unit, a good group, consisted of about 75 medical doctors, of all specialities, at least two dozen nurses, all female, and about 150 enlisted men, and non-commissioned officers. It was a hairy time: things were going on around us in our country which brought consternation to the young and the old, with revolutions going on in our music, our relations with the drug scene, VietNam and its entanglements, even what would later be called and conducted the Second Vatican Council and its gift to the Church and the world.

I was a 33-year-old Cajun priest stationed at Our Lady of Lourdes church in Violet, with its five missions, assigned to Our Lady of the Rosary Church in New Orleans that year, with Bishop Abel Caillouet as my pastor. The Army sent me to Chaplain School in New Rochelle, New York for a second stint, with the rank of Captain. By that time, I was fairly familiar with the members of the Unit—most from New Orleans and its environs, having attended summer camp at Fort Polk, Louisiana every year.

One evening at the Officers' Club, I got into a conversation with one of the doctors, Dr. Jerry Patten, a well-read and practicing Catholic. During our talk, he informed me that he had run into a newly-published book by James A. Michener, named The Source. It was quite long but was extremely well done and named to receive a Pulitzer Prize for Literature, and how he loved it. I didn't know much about the book, but it would touch and color my life, even if I had heard very little about it before.

The Source is structured as a story that contains 13 stories within it. Each of the stories builds in chronological order on the last. What struck me most closely was what it did in the anthropology it opened up for me. And, as I read it in fascination, it opened for me the whole concept of Sacred Scripture as the Bible emerged from the early history of humankind to our own time. It is a work of genius—still in publication, in print and audiobooks. It still fascinates me—I have it in my library in both forms.

My study of Scripture before that was quite thorough, with good teachers, fine reading and study. But this novel gave me not only a direction to go into with my own thought and reading, but it set the context of what I had already learned into what would benefit me in my own preaching and into further study, with a Masters in Religious Education at Loyola in 1976, capped later on with a visit to the Holy Land, in 1982.

And from that occasion since then, I have been not only immersed by Holy Scripture, but I've been involved in teaching it and have responded to the Roman Catholic thirst for reading the Bible which we today find in our people. I, too, have that thirst—in my reading, my study, and my life as a priest. And I deplore the neglect of our urgency for our people to have read the Bible when I was younger. It is a study well worth our attention, our thought and our reading not only the Bible itself but whatever we can find about the Word of God in our time and place. And to a large extent, <u>The Source</u> helped me move into this attention which I now have: and I am grateful for that pursuit of this Word.

## STORY 75: Best Friend, Growing Up: Still in Contact?

Our high school graduation class at St. Joseph's in New Roads had 12 in it: 6 boys and 6 girls. Of those six boys (this was in 1946: we were graduating from the 11th grade), five of us were close—all altar boys, 4-H Club, basketball team, band, and football (when we could find uniforms and pads!). A good group, remarked upon by the town mayor in praise at our graduation. And of this group, T Morel and I were the closest, I thought.

Of course, "boys don't have best friends—girls do!" So, we didn't call our friendship that, but we were close. T Morel was valedictorian, and I was next in line in our class. We did so much together—we hunted, talked about life, sailed on False River, swam together with the bunch, and went to school together. And together we braved it through those terrible "hormones" challenges. I hope I never go through such a patch again—we were curious about girls, sex, and love, but always at a distance. At least, it was for me in my innocence.

Already by the end of grammar school, I was headed for the seminary, even if I waited until graduation to enter it. T Morel was much more involved and experienced with girls and on a much more intimate way; I found out later on. I now think that this for him moved us from our closeness as we moved into our separate ways. After graduation, he entered the Navy, earned the GI Bill, and entered LSU to study medicine, while I entered St. Ben's seminary. He was the youngest of four, and I was the oldest of four—a real difference.

To show the distance between our attitudes, let me recall. T Morel's brother was a great pianist and was stationed here in Algiers, in the Navy, but on weekends, he would play in one of those piano lounges in the French Quarter. He came home on leave one weekend, and T Morel and I drove him back to the city on Sunday evening. He showed us where he regularly played, and then we headed up Bourbon Street "to see what we could see."

Ahead of us (and I was not at all comfortable, seeing the pictures of those scantily clad ladies! Spiritual books called that "custody of the eyes") I could see a crowd of people clustered around the doorway of one of the bars. And Felix told T Morel, "You're going to like this—come on, I know this stripper." And we joined the crowded doorway, until I looked up and saw this woman dancing around WITH NOTHING ON BUT A TINY THING AT HER WAIST! "Chere Pichee!"

Well, I couldn't stay in that crowd, so I backed out of the place. If I could have washed out my eyes, I would have gladly done so. I waited outside on the street until they joined me. They asked me why I didn't go in with them, and, ashamed I think, I told them that I had been moved by the crowd past the doorway. It wasn't true—but I wouldn't have told them that I wanted to be somewhere else—this might be a sin! And this was the difference between me, my upbringing, and my direction and T Morel. But I didn't realize that until much later.

He became an Anesthesiologist, had a family, and moved to Santa Barbara, California where his third daughter could have a good schooling in her handicap: I admired that. But from his wedding on (where I had officiated), we moved into two directions—he with his medicine and life and I in several parishes. When I anointed his father-in-law, we reunited, but it wasn't the same—he teased me about how much I was talking (because I was so glad to see him and his wife, but he wasn't interested in our being close). I now see that I was closer to him than he was to me. I still admire him, but my vision of our friendship is now more realistic. He was a gift to me as we were growing up, and I am grateful for what my life was in our younger days.

## STORY 76: "Me and the 'Il Faut' Concept"

In all the "lore" that Cajuns have to contend with, "Il Faut" is a very strong one, affecting our lives daily as we encounter life in its many dimensions. It's been called by many names: routine, obligation, daily living, personal habits, or "you gotta" to name a few.

And, as I face my retirement this summer, I'm beginning to reflect upon these realities and how my life will be affected. For one thing, "Il Faut" will become a part of my life, not from the outside, but from my own decisions, my own responsibilities, and how I choose to live my life in retirement, at least in the beginning, at the Villa for retired priests here on the West Bank. Sometimes it seems to look challenging, quite enticing, maybe uncomfortable: but at this time, a very new position for me. I'm not sure how I feel about it—it certainly will mean a change for me.

From what I've seen and experienced, the Archdiocese has been very respectful and grateful to us priests, especially during the reign of Archbishop Greg Aymond. Always thankful to the priests for their dedication and years of priestly service, he has bent over backward to help us in our ministry in ways I've never experienced in the past (and I've experienced five of them: Archbps Rummel, Hannan, Schulte, and Hughes). There has been in the past (and still is today in some quarters) a sort of triumphalism. You were always at a distance from the "little folks"—the people in the pews, almost on another plane of life, above.

Today, there is much more an openness and a recognition of the value of the foibles and the downright ordinariness of life as we try to live it in the Church. (At the Vatican II Council, we read, "The joys and the hopes, the griefs and the anxieties of the men of this age, especially those who are poor or in any way afflicted, these too are the joys and hopes, the griefs and anxieties of the followers of Christ. Indeed, nothing genuinely human fails to raise an echo in their hearts. For theirs is a community composed of men (and women). United in Christ, they are led by the Holy Spirit in their journey to the kingdom of their Father, and they have welcomed the news of salvation which is meant for every man" ("Gaudium et Spes"—Preface of the Pastoral Constitution of the Church in the Modern World).

We wonder these days, "What do we have to do to attract more youngsters (or oldsters, for that matter) to the Priesthood and religious life, men and women?" In the old days, the seminary and convent classes were overflowing. Today, we rejoice when we hear that we have "55 seminarians in the whole seminary." In 1946, we had that many in only a single class!

There are many memories I have of the old days—when the prime virtue we pursued was obedience. There was little emphasis on creativity, autonomy, decision-making, consensus-building, maturity. One took instructions from superiors (because "you were an inferior"!). In a sense, we were to be led by the hand because we had no right to make any serious decision or choice, unless we were told. This has changed greatly in the past decades. "Il faut" no longer rides triumphantly.

So, as I look toward retirement (and this is a new reality for me), I've never really thought about how old I was, nor about my retirement. O, yes, I've invested in the IRA's, gotten a Variable Annuity, and even the insurance we were advised to get. But what would it be like for you—yes, you!—that which only now has come to be real for me. I pray for the wisdom, the patience, and the courage which I will need to be what God continues to call me to be, even when I can sleep as long as I want, or stay home when I want to stay home. Certainly, it will be another interesting phase of my life.

## STORY 77: "You Knew You Were in Trouble when . . . ."

It happened as I was coming out of serious surgery at West Jeff Hospital several years ago. Barbara and Richard Donlon had driven me to the hospital and were a great help to me during the whole affair.

The surgery went well—I was wheeled out of surgery to the recovery room and then the next day to the ICU, with all its beeps, bells, and boops. I had spent a night of the usual sensations and wondered where we were, and what would happen. It was an interesting experience.

I was relieved to see the Donlons at the foot of my bed when I woke that morning. The usual question, "How are you feeling?" "Fine, I'm OK, thank God." Then my two nurses came in with the breakfast tray and began preparing me. It was then that I realized that I was in trouble: when I uncovered the breakfast plate, I could feel the nausea coming up. What to do? Quick, grab that cover and try to contain it all. It wasn't enough. Niagara Falls.

Most ungraciously, I threw up on the cover, the tray, and some even splashed as far as Barbara! I was so embarrassed, but what happened after that made it one of the funniest experiences I've ever had!

Without batting an eye, she stood up, looked at the two nurses standing there and told them (and me), "This is what it means to be retired. Clean him up!" And turned around and left the room. Which they did so well, in spite of my expressions of remorse (as if it had never happened before).

This moved me to commend those two nurses to the Director of Nursing at the Hospital for their care and professionalism. They took such good care, and, today, I'm healthy. And as for Barbara, her sense of humor still stands her well. God bless her, our teacher.

## STORY 78: ANOTHER THRESHOLD

I have found a recurring reality as I go through my life and my age levels: we go through many ending/beginning experiences into different, and perhaps new, statuses where we run into life and its changed demands of us. This may sound very abstract with the fuzziness of the personal experience of someone who doesn't know how to describe that experience. Let me try to explain.

In the year before I graduated from high school, it frequently crossed my mind that, by the time the next year would come around, my life would be so drastically changed from what it had been for several years. A new school, a new schedule, a new place, new demands of me, new friends—all different from what they had been. Not threatening, but a challenge to how I would live my life in a whole new plane. And I would have to cross some sort of threshold to get there.

That has happened so many times since then: different times, different places, and different people—all good and enriching my life as I age and embrace what I feel is God's will and providence for me.

Some of these challenges have dealt with my life and what I could not foresee. My first assignment (with two other priests older than I) taught me a great deal, about experience and what being a priest-in-a-parish would mean for my future. And it was good. Later on, there would be many challenges of many sorts: different pastors, different parishes, and different people (from Islenos in St. Bernard to Cajuns in Terrebonne Parish, to "Yats" in the city). And now, another threshold: moving to retirement from active ministry as a pastor and continuing to live as retired on the West Bank.

The prospect contains little uncertainty for me except for an openness to what God's will is going to demand. And it is all pleasant (except for the affection and generosity that Holy Spirit people will show by including some sort of farewell occasion, which will not be easy after 38 years of our association and growth together). I have made such great friendships.

For the present, as I look toward that threshold, I don't think that I can anticipate very much other than a good setting with seven other retired priests who, as I hope to do, help in the parishes of the Archdiocese with ministry. There my life will take a different sort of direction, even if I know that there will be little difference from my present schedule of praying, reading, meeting people, and, in gratitude, enjoying my life which has been such a good one.

I hope and pray that the many friendships given to me will continue and blossom as we spend our time left in gratitude, humor, fun, and peace. Ain't life grand?

# STORY 79: A Great Sign of Faith and Discipline

There are many stories to be told these days when we think about those 33 miners in Chile who were rescued last week. It is said that they come from impoverished areas and have their own stories to tell. But for us in the New Orleans area, one reality stands out: their deep, strong, disciplined life and the faith which carried them up to safety, and the success of their rescuers in achieving that goal.

It is said that their leader foresaw what they faced for the first 17 days and took it upon himself and his peers to put order into their time of waiting for rescue, even if they knew not whether someone was aware of the situation or could reach them in time. For those two and a half weeks, their plight in that cave became international news, and, in that time, they were organized into squads to make their cave-in space livable. They had food and water for only a couple of days as they took shelter together. A spoonful of tuna and a sip of water: their supplies would enable them to survive for only 48 hours!

Their spaces were organized—a space for toilet; a space for exercise; a space for rest; and a space for prayer. Their time was organized: all of the group was divided into activities which would carry them into looking to the future, even though they had no idea if anyone knew about them or would be able to extend any rescue effort. No thought about panic (that we know of), or suicide, or even cannibalism (stories about a plane wreck years ago in the Andes made that a possibility). And all of them were brought up back into their lives.

We watched as the rescue capsule came into view, bringing them out one by one amid cheers ("Chi, Chi, Chi; Le!, Le!, Le!") from the people on the surface as the world watched. We even were able to watch as, in the bottom of the mine, one by one they entered the capsule for the 15 minute ride up to safety.

What a very patent sign of what faith can do when people are disciplined enough to trust that help was coming their way, and the patience it took to enable them to last it through. Whatever was in their minds and hearts we can only surmise. The thoroughness of their planning—it was even agreed upon by the group that whatever profit would be achieved from their stories (in books and films) would be divided among themselves in the future.

Of course, the "comedy masters of the night" and their television viewers would find material to squeeze "humor" out of the group, in the northern hemisphere. What was abundantly clear was our view of the faces of these men as they emerged, encased in the steel capsule as it was drawn up by that wheel turning to bring them up one by one. There was no gloom or panic, but a quiet, steady, relief on their faces, and the joy which ensued as they were rejoined with their loved ones. One even emerged to get down on his knees in grateful prayer for all of us to see.

The triumph of faith and the human spirit which extended beyond fear, uncertainty, impossibility, and anxiety. We can learn much from them. God be with them, and us.

## STORY 80: An Unusual Stance

This is a story told by Tony Majoria. He and Peggy were at the home of his son, Ron, in Baton Rouge. While Tony was seated on the edge of the pool and speaking with the family members around the pool, he didn't notice Katie, the granddaughter. seated next to him. At five years old, she was painting her toenails a deep purple. After a while, Tony saw that, while he was speaking and listening to the family members, Katie had begun to paint his toenails, too.

Turning to Katie, he told her, "No, honey, not Paw-pa's nails—just do yours. And you're doing such a good job!"

She got up and returned to the kitchen. And he thought that was the end of the matter. What he didn't notice was that she had painted only the nails on one foot, which was quite significant.

A few days later, Tony was back home in English Turn. Early one morning he had on his robe but no shoes as he went outside to get his morning newspaper. When he picked up the paper, he was greeted by Will Lannes, his next-door neighbor, a long-time friend. And they got into a conversation about current affairs. The conversation lasted about an hour, and Tony returned to the house. He said that it didn't enter his mind about his appearance as he spoke with Will, heading inside to have his morning coffee.

It was only later, as he thought about it, that he realized that he had stood around his mailbox speaking with Will and that he was barefooted, with the nails painted on his left foot only, painted a deep purple! So, he called up Will and told him, "Will, I know that you noticed my feet while we were talking the other day. My granddaughter had painted them and did only one foot. I'm sure that you wondered what that was about."

Will's response was, "No, Tony, I didn't notice it." Tony said that this was a sign of Will's courteous nature—he HAD to have noticed and wondered about the nails and the fact that only one foot was painted. And he was too much of a gentleman to remark about it. Tony has a good laugh about the whole thing—and I think that perhaps it is true that Will didn't notice, but it was a very funny scenario.

## STORY 81: "Ye Olde Hoof in Mouth"

In 1981, when our new church was being dedicated, we had a very full church with visiting priests and Archbishop Hannan, who had arranged for the Archdiocese of New Orleans to buy the two and a half acres from the Jesuit Fathers to finally build our parish facilities. We had planned what sort of building we needed; we had interviewed architects and contractors and decided on our plans.

At the time, we were still at St. Philip's Episcopal Church, down the street, and did our interviews there. Very businesslike. We had been established for almost ten years, and our life still was fraught with difficulties: being in someone's else's church, only a few parish families, a large Vietnamese contingent, a health crisis (no voice for me), and an uncertain future. But we forged on.

Finally, we were built, both the church building and the rectory. And the Archbishop had come to dedicate the building. After all the liturgical ceremonies were coming to a close, I as pastor came to the pulpit to make concluding remarks before the reception (which would also take place in the church—it was primarily a gathering place for our people—a place to pray, a place to play, and a place to stay). We were home, at last! No more "Quousque tamen, Domine?—How long, O Lord?"

At the microphone, I was walking three feet off the floor—excitement, joy, pride, and gratitude oozing from every pore! My remarks will always haunt me.

"Today, we celebrate so much. We have wandered far and wide; we have welcomed so many people who have truly been our brothers and sisters into our community. And this includes in a special way the people of St. Philip's Episcopal Church who have been so Christian in their hospitality to us for so many years when we had nowhere else to go.

In a special way, we want to recognize and thank the Archdiocese of New Orleans who made all this possible. And especially I want to thank Archbishop Rummel, here with us today and who has been a special 'Father' to us." And I stopped—what a gaffe! What do I do? ["Just don't stop talking—you've already got your foot in your mouth. Don't quit now!"] Then I said those immortal words, "You're not Archbishop Rummel; you're Archbishop Hannan and from the bottom of my heart, I thank you!" Laughter and applause. And relief, I thought.

I have never forgotten that moment and how red-faced I was, but, by that time, I didn't care—the fat was in the fire, so let it burn. Archbishop Hannan (who is now 98 years old) has never brought it up again, for which I am grateful, and I would like to let the whole incident fade into oblivion, except when I remember it. And I still am grateful for all of God's gifts. The song, "I know the plans I have for you," says the Lord: "plans of fullness and not of harm . . . to give you a future and a hope!" How true.

## STORY 82: "The 2011 Mississippi River Flood"

As we watch the rapidly rising Mississippi river, there is consternation all around. Many areas north of us are already flooded, and it is only the middle of May. There have been some frequent and heavy snows and rains, and already the Bonne Carre Spillway has been opened to relieve the pressure on our levees. Now, today the Morganza Control Structure was also opened with the worry of the people living in the floodway, including Morgan City and parts of St. Landry and Terrebonne parishes. It has been decided that massive amounts of water will pour through that structure.

When we hear about the Morganza Control Structure, it brings to mind my own involvement in its construction and how it touched our lives in the early 1950's. I was in Notre Dame Seminary in my third year there that summer vacation. Daddy told us about a Corps of Engineers man who came by the shop and asked if we could work with them to remedy a situation they were encountering as they prepared to build a bridge in the Morganza Spillway. Their "forms" had come in damaged: these were the 10 foot long steel forms, weighing over 500 pounds, 350 of them. They would need to be trucked into the shop, a steel brace cut, and then the bent parts would be pressed straight and then welded.

These forms were needed to build the long pilings to be driven deeply into the ground to support the bridge which contains the slips which raise or lower the bays which contain or permit the river water through to flow down toward the Gulf, hundreds of miles south. A massive job: it would involve me, my two brothers, Daddy, of course, and several men who lived near the shop in New Roads, 10 miles from Morganza. A whole process to take us months to finish.

We took on the job and did a good job of it. We called it our "assembly line," and all did it with zest, including me, the seminarian. When the last of the forms had been worked on, we rejoiced in a job well done.

Now when I think of that Spillway Control Structure, I remember that it did touch my life and enabled Daddy and Mom to have a new house built next door to the shop, and it remains there today. Daddy lived about 15 years after that, and Mom lived there many years: she told me once, "Daddy and I were so happy there in our new house of which we were so proud."

Jerry and I have spoken about that job as we recalled what we had done, and how we had worked together to build that structure, and how we had done so well, that our folks could have a nice house which was such a real home for us. And now today, we hear all the news about how important for the state and the country to have the river relieve the pressure on the cities south of Morganza and their levees.

"O Lord, have mercy on us, and spare us from flooding, storms and natural disasters. Be with the folks who will suffer from the high water and its flooding effects already occurring."

## STORY 83: "Renovabis Faciem Terrae"?

The first parish assignment given me in 1954 was a good one to help me into parish work and parish life. The pastor was a very talented Cajun priest (piano-player, Officialis on the Tribunal, and Consultor in the diocese); his niece was housekeeper and a toughie; Bill Greene the other assistant: a friend. This parish was the only parish, in the days before evening Vigil Masses and air-conditioning, which had a 3:00 Sunday morning Fisherman's Mass, always well-attended.

"The Monsignor" was a man easy to get along with, but the housekeeper, his niece, kept tabs on us and did her reporting to him. One of his rules was that whenever there was a child's funeral among our families (and he very seldom took any funerals), we were not to go to the family home to bless and bring the body to the church for the funeral. (I still have no idea why this was.)

Anyway, one of the very active families in the parish had twins, one of whom got very ill and died, perhaps at no more than two years of age. The family was devastated. I had visited the boy several times and anointed him in the hospital. When he died, I had to make a decision: would I do what the Monsignor ruled, or would I do what my conscience told me to do—go to their home and bring him to the church? Which is what I decided to do.

After the funeral and burial had been completed and I was entering the kitchen, I met the housekeeper. She informed me that she had told "my uncle and he's going to fix your a—!" So I knew what was coming—with dismay.

When I entered his room, he was reading a National Geographic magazine and angrily told me, "I hear that you went and did what you knew I didn't want you to do with that baby funeral. I want to know something—at your ordination, did you take a vow to "Renovabis Faciem Terrae"? I didn't know how to respond to that. First thing—I wanted to bust our laughing at this way of fussing at me. But I didn't dare.

All I could muster was to stammer and tell him, "I'm sorry, Monsignor, I felt that this was the right thing to do. You know I will not disobey you, but this family deserved that we support them in their grieving over this dead child. It won't happen again." As to his question, after all these almost sixty years later, I still find to be priceless. In those days, we prayed to the Holy Spirit on Pentecost this prayer: "Domine, emitte Spiritum Sanctum," with the response, "Et renovabis faciem terrae," which means, "Lord, send down your Holy Spirit, and you will renew the face of the earth."

Still, it was a most surprising question for him to ask me. And, today I still laugh about it, and, YES, I did take that vow when I was ordained. "Come, Holy Spirit."

## In closing . . .

"I know the plans I have for you," says the Lord, "plans of fullness and not of harm . . . to give you a future and a hope!"

Jeremiah 29:11 ff

Each day these words continue to give me support and hope during my (our) journey.

*   *   *

CPSIA information can be obtained at www.ICGtesting.com
Printed in the USA
BVOW05*0734230315

392257BV00016B/109/P